William Cunningham

The Use and Abuse of Money

William Cunningham

The Use and Abuse of Money

ISBN/EAN: 9783743317390

Manufactured in Europe, USA, Canada, Australia, Japa

Cover: Foto ©ninafisch / pixelio.de

Manufactured and distributed by brebook publishing software
(www.brebook.com)

William Cunningham

The Use and Abuse of Money

UNIVERSITY EXTENSION MANUALS

EDITED BY PROFESSOR KNIGHT

THE USE AND ABUSE

OF

MONEY

OF

MONEY

BY

W. CUNNINGHAM, D.D.

VICAR OF GREAT ST. MARY'S, AND UNIVERSITY LECTURER, CAMBRIDGE

NEW YORK

CHARLES SCRIBNER'S SONS

1891

PREFACE.

—•—

THIS book is intended for those who are already familiar with the outlines of the subject, and it is meant to help them to think on topics about which everybody talks. Primers and elementary manuals of economic science usually make a general assumption about human nature, and take for granted that man is actuated by a single motive,—the desire of wealth. But if we examine in greater detail the personal qualities and various motives that influence conduct in regard to economic affairs, we shall obtain a more complete explanation of the observed phenomena, and we shall also be better able to bring our knowledge to bear on actual occurrences.

I cannot hope that those who read this *Manual* will agree with all the conclusions reached. It deals throughout with subjects on which there are many conflicting opinions, and it deals with them from a single and well-defined standpoint. It aims at working towards a consistent treatment of social difficulties, not by propounding any new doctrine, but by recognising that each of the conflicting doctrines has some elements of truth, and by suggesting the questions How far, and within what limits is this opinion true?

The subject discussed is *Capital in its Relation to Social Progress*. When first entering on economic studies we are advised to lay aside all other matters, and confine our attention to wealth as something we can isolate from other social phenomena. And this is the simplest way to begin and the best way to go on for examining some problems, but not for examining all. It is necessary for some purposes to look at these matters in another way, and to consider an economic force, not apart from, but in its relation to the other sides of human life and interest. In the present day, when Capital dominates in so many directions, it is not uninteresting to select this particular factor, and consider the part which Capital has played and its bearing on the material progress of the race. Thus we shall traverse a field which affords us an opportunity of surveying the strong positions occupied by modern socialists.

But though this is its subject, the book is called, *The Use and Abuse of Money*. I wish to lay stress on the element of personal responsibility. Much has been written about the duties of landowners, and it seems worth while to say a little about the responsibilities of moneyed men for the manner in which they employ their capital and spend their income. When people discuss economic matters as if the changes were due to a play

of forces that act on men and so impel men, the importance of the part played by the man himself is obscured.
Man in his highest aspects, and the best of all he does,
is not susceptible of thorough treatment by economic
science, so long as it concentrates attention on the play
of measurable motive forces. As has been well said,
'much of the best work of the world has no price, and
evades altogether the economic calculus.' Mill's great
achievement as an economist was in his attempt to
combine a careful study of the higgling of the market
with a full recognition of the importance of the nobler
elements in human nature, and a study of the increase
of wealth with discussions of the improvement of society.
Though recent economists have done much to correct
his solution of particular problems, it is not clear that
they have been wise in deliberately rejecting the example he set them of bringing into prominence 'the human
as opposed to the mechanical element in economics.'
The present sketch simply follows out some of the suggestions made by Mill, with the view of raising the
question, *Whether a full recognition of the human element in economics may not be the best means of attaining
to clear definitions of economic terms, and to the distinct
statement and thorough discussion of fundamental economic
problems?*

As one of the pioneers of the University Extension
Movement in 1874, I found great advantage in providing a careful syllabus. I have thought it worth while
to prefix a similar syllabus to this *Manual.* It mentions
the names of several books which will enable readers

to pursue their studies further; but I have not insisted on burdening the pages of a popular treatise with detailed references to authorities in regard to every matter of fact to which allusion is made.

W. C.

TRINITY COLLEGE, CAMBRIDGE,
November, 1890.

SYLLABUS OF THE SUBJECT AND BOOKS FOR REFERENCE.

—•■•—

PART I.

SOCIAL PROBLEMS.

—•■•—

CHAPTER I.

POLITICAL ECONOMY WITH ASSUMPTIONS AND WITHOUT.

I.

1. Adam Smith made an advance on his predecessors, because he did not discuss the maintenance of national power, but concentrated attention on one element—wealth. He stated the problems regarding political prosperity in a more general form than either mercantilists, physiocrats, or other writers had done . *Page* 1

2. He assumed the existing social order and current motives. Most economists have followed him in taking for granted the facts of human nature and of the physical world. Mill, *Political Economy*, p. 13 2

II.

For some purposes it is convenient to start with such assumptions, but,

1. It is difficult to make the most convenient assumption about changing nature, and still more so to state precisely what has been assumed. Mill, *Political Economy*, II, iv. § 1 . . . 4

2. It may be confusing, since it is not easy to divest ourselves of these fundamental assumptions when we try to do so, as our very language involves them 5

3. It is disappointing to find that we have made so little advance towards the scientific treatment of questions which lie beyond our assumptions, and require us to recognise changes in human nature itself 6

CHAPTER II.

INDUSTRY WITHOUT CAPITAL.

I.

II.

III.

CHAPTER III.

CAPITALIST ERA.

I.

The Capitalist Era in England.

CHAPTER IV.

MATERIAL PROGRESS AND MORAL INDIFFERENCE.

I.

II.

CHAPTER V.

THE CONTROL OF CAPITAL.

I.

PART II.
PRACTICAL QUESTIONS.

—•—

CHAPTER VI.

THE FORMATION OF CAPITAL.

I.

3

CHAPTER VII.

THE INVESTMENT OF CAPITAL.

I.

III.

CHAPTER VIII.

CAPITAL IN ACTION.

I.

II.

CHAPTER IX.

THE REPLACEMENT OF CAPITAL.

I.

II.

CHAPTER X.

THE DIRECTION OF CAPITAL.

I.

PART III.

PERSONAL DUTY.

—•—

CHAPTER XI.

PERSONAL RESPONSIBILITY.

CHAPTER XII.

DUTY IN REGARD TO EMPLOYING CAPITAL.

III.

CHAPTER XIII.

DUTY IN REGARD TO THE RETURN ON CAPITAL.

I.

II.

III.

CHAPTER XIV.

THE ENJOYMENT OF WEALTH.

I.

PART I.

SOCIAL PROBLEMS.

CHAPTER I.

Political Economy with Assumptions and Without.

I. Assumptions made by Adam Smith and others.

1. Adam Smith's greatness as an economist is very striking when we compare the *Wealth of Nations* with the works of his predecessors, and see what he did. It is still more striking when we compare his book with the writings of those who have followed him, and see how little they have accomplished in the way of amplifying his work, and supplying what he left undone. We may recognise the importance of Malthus, Ricardo, and Jevons; they have given us fresh light on particular doctrines, as to population or rent or value; but the fact remains that the *Wealth of Nations* is not only read as a classic, but is still used as a text book of the whole subject.

Adam Smith left his predecessors behind, because he gave a new turn to the old enquiries. The statesmen and politicians of different nations had been each trying to work out a practical problem; each had enquired how to develop the resources of his own country in such fashion as to promote the power of that state. The problem had taken one shape in Germany with its petty principalities, and administrative science. It had taken another form in France with its great agricultural resources, and physiocratic doctrine.   It had taken yet another in England with its facilities for commerce, and mercantile system.   Adam Smith stated the matter in a more general form than any of these writers had done by concentrating attention on wealth,—something which was required in all these different countries alike.   The first books of his great work really deal with a topic which might be regarded as of common interest to all nations; it is only in the last books that questions of policy, of using the wealth for the support of the state, come into prominence.   The old writers began with power and worked back to the sinews of power; they were politicians first, financiers next, and economists last of all.   Adam Smith felt that wealth could be dealt with apart from considerations of political power; he treated the subject in a more abstract fashion, and also in such a manner that his results were of more general application.   He attacked the mercantilists chiefly, but he superseded the German school and the physiocrats as well. So much for what he did.

2. But he left much undone, for he classified the different topics with which he dealt in a rough and ready fashion; he never stated precisely what he assumed, and he took the phenomena of society as the ordinary superficial observer recognised them.   It was clear to him that even the poor in civilised countries 'enjoy a greater share of the necessaries and conveniences of life than it is possible for any savage to acquire.'   He finds that the chief reason for this lies in the larger 'proportion of useful labour,' and that the large number of useful labourers is due to the 'quantity of capital stock which is employed in setting them to work.'   But he simply took these factors, as they were familiarly known in England in the eighteenth century, and traced out their working; he hardly set himself to resolve them into their elements, physical and personal.   He never explicitly recognises that the free labourer is the product of a highly complicated civilisation, and that capital is only found in small quantities, if at all, among savage or backward peoples.

Adam Smith might have tried to trace the genesis of both

of these factors in the production of wealth; but for his immediate object it was not necessary to do so. He was writing a book for the English public in the hope of accomplishing a practical reform, and in that object he succeeded beyond his highest expectations. Had he aimed at mere formal correctness he might never have caught public attention, and he exercised a wise discretion in avoiding scholastic precision. Perhaps the very greatness of his success has prevented others from thoroughly investigating the facts and principles which he assumed; his followers have done much in re-stating truths for modern society in better terms and with greater precision, but they have been inclined to imitate him by accepting, as normal, phenomena which only show themselves in a highly complicated society.

Modern economists like Mill assume the 'facts of human nature and of the physical world,' and postulate them as the basis of the science; but after all this basis is not secure, for the facts of human nature are continually changing. It is not very convenient to fix on any one type of character to the exclusion of the rest, at least for enquiries that have to do with distant places or distant times. If we take the average nineteenth century Englishman,—and how shall we strike that average?—but if we take him as typical, it will not be easy to apply any of the results we reach to a country inhabited by Hindus, for we do not know how to make the necessary corrections. There is a similar difficulty even in drawing on our modern experience for explanations of industrial changes in by-gone days in England. Human nature is very complicated and is constantly changing, and we seem to narrow the range of our enquiry unnecessarily if we confine our attention to a single type. How and when are we to deal with the other types?

It might appear at all events that we may assume the facts of the physical world as constant; the changes in the material universe are so slow that the phenomena may be regarded as permanent when compared with the duration of human life on the globe. But this is scarcely so; for economic purposes the consideration which is important is generally speaking, not what physical nature is, but how far it is understood.   As men increase in their knowledge of physical facts and in their power over them, the industrial and commercial character of the physical world wears a different aspect.   There is no range of acquaintance with physical nature and no definite type of human character which remains unmodified for many generations in any period of progress, and it is inconvenient to have to assume some definite range and definite type when we are discussing the causes and the course of material progress.

II.   Difficulty of Stating and of Working from these Assumptions.

1. That this is a real difficulty might be seen more clearly if we were to review the various attempts that economists have made to state the precise assumptions they are making. Nothing can be of greater importance than that the fundamental assumptions, the very basis of all subsequent discussion, should be clearly stated; but the difficulty of doing this well appears to be insuperable.   Thus it is common for economists to assume free competition, and Mill seems to hold that economic phenomena cannot be scientifically investigated without the aid of this assumption; but there is very great difficulty in stating precisely what it means.   Some writers scarcely attempt to define it, while others would tell us that the phrase ' free competition ' describes a state of society when every man pursues ' a course which, without entering into combination with others, he has deliberately selected as that which is likely to be of the greatest material advantage to himself and his family.' The assumption of free competition in this form may be fairly convenient for dealing with many commercial questions, but it is ludicrously unsatisfactory as a means of approaching the examination of the struggle between organised labour and capital.   Yet it would be very difficult to restate the definition so as to include competing associations and corporations as

well as competing individuals. The consideration of this single instance may show that while it is often useful to proceed by the help of assumptions, there is a double difficulty with which we have to contend; on the one hand it is very hard to think out the particular hypothesis we shall assume, and on the other it is very hard to state precisely what we are taking for granted.

2. There is, however, another point of view from which we can see the difficulties which attend this method of procedure. Unless we know what we have assumed and can state it quite clearly, we may fail to divest ourselves of these presuppositions, even when we try to do so. Thus, as has been noticed above, Adam Smith assumed existing social arrangements and classes—landlords, capitalists and labourers—in his treatise, and other economists have followed him in this; even in cases where the assumption appears to be laid aside, it is still implicitly present. Economists, when describing the growth of industry or commerce, are not always ready to face the real problem and examine the change from savagery to civilisation as it has actually taken place in any part of the world; they appeal instead to the probable experience of a Robinson Crusoe,—a man with all the industrial habits and modes of thinkings of a modern Englishman. These fancy illustrations tell us at best what a modern Englishman would try to do if he found himself in an isolated position, or when he came in friendly contact with savages; but they do not throw any light on the question as to the steps by which a primitive people, with no ideas of exchange and no habits of saving, emerges from barbarism. So long as the terminology of economics is framed on a rough and ready scheme drawn from the phenomena of modern society, our treatment of history is necessarily superficial, because, by the language we use, we read into primitive times the very habits and practices of which we profess to trace the origin and growth.

A similar defect may even be detected in the writings of some of those who have ranged themselves in opposition to the existing order, and desire to introduce something very different. The Labour and Capital of which they write are still Labour and Capital as known in modern society; the communist would reconstruct all the conditions of life, but he appears to assume that Labour could be directed and controlled, in these new circumstances, as effectively or more effectively than it is at present. The motives to work, the manner of work, the training for work, would all be altered; it is a complicated speculation to guess how Labour would be affected by these changes. Could society count upon laborious drudgery being regularly done if effect were given to the great principle of the gratuitousness of service? It is a large assumption, (whether it is a justifiable one or not), and it sometimes seems to creep in by mere implication, when language framed in accordance with the present state, is used to describe the possible economic conditions in some future Utopia. Just as some economists are apt to be superficial when they write of the past, because their language makes use of the very things they profess to explain, so other economists are apt to be superficial when they write of the future because their language implies the retention, under changed circumstances, of much that might have passed away.

3. There is a further inconvenience in basing the whole of our scientific treatment on some particular assumption about human nature. In so far as the assumption fails us we are left without any help for conducting a reasoned and scientific investigation. It may be the most convenient, or even the only possible, mode for treating certain modern problems, when we can be sure that human beings will continue to be the same for all practical purposes. For short periods, during which there is no modification in human habits, it may answer admirably; but where human motives change in character, or human habits are altered, our fundamental assumption becomes untrue, and we have no scientific means of correcting our results, so as to make them apply to the changed condition. The inadequacy of ordinary economic reasoning has been brought to light during the last decade, when attention has been increasingly directed to social problems which force us to recognise the fact that there have

been and may be fundamental changes in human nature itself. There is at present a wide-spread dissatisfaction with the existing social order, and schemes for mending it, or even for ending it, are eagerly welcomed in many quarters. There is also an increasing interest in the social life of bygone days, or of primitive peoples, and the diffusion of 'village communities,' whether free or not, and of gilds of different types, has impressed the popular imagination; but for describing the practice of these bodies in detail our ordinary economic terminology does not serve satisfactorily. There is another reason for pushing our examination a little further than was done by Adam Smith and has been accepted by his successors. In taking modern English society as normal they found a plain, but not high, view of the relations of morality to commerce. They found that some kinds of conduct were prohibited by law, and that certain actions were commonly regarded as discreditable breaches of business etiquette, but they did not raise questions of right and wrong within these wide limits. Those who hope to elevate the public standard, to distinguish fairness from unfairness in different transactions, are forced to try and find distinctions which are commonly ignored—that is to say, they must try to analyse more minutely.

The rough and ready acceptance of modern society as normal, and of its phenomena as typical, serves for the discussion of practical fiscal questions in the present or immediate future. There is an immense number of problems connected with currency and finance and tariffs which can be conveniently dealt with on the ordinary assumptions; but there are others, and these for the most part are wider and more important questions, which can only be treated satisfactorily when they are examined in another light. Those who are anxious to understand the history of the past, or to raise the tone of commercial morality, or to forecast the course of society, will not be satisfied to look at all economic questions through the medium of modern society, or with the aid of any assumption about the dominant factors in human nature,

Since economic science assumes a certain type of human nature, its results simply become irrelevant if we wish to understand a long period of the past, during which human nature has been altering, or to forecast a future, in which, as we hope, human nature will be different from what it is now. The principles that economists have formulated, the terms they use, cannot be applied directly and easily to the changed conditions; in order to apply them at all we should have to enter on a different kind of enquiry,—to analyse human nature more carefully, to state how far e. g. the nature of the Hindu in a village community corresponds to, and how far it differs from, the type of human nature we have assumed, and to see what probabilities there are that it can be modified to any great extent in a given time. It is only after some such investigation that we can attempt to apply the principles of economic science in regions where our fundamental assumptions about human nature do not hold good. Unless there is a serious effort to do something of the sort, our treatment of the widest and deepest economic problems must be entirely haphazard, as it will depend on the fashion in which our sentiments or our fancies induce us to discard, or to retain, the conclusions which had been accurately worked out for a different state of affairs. A pessimist writer will take one view, an optimist another; there can be no argument between them, because neither has any means of giving a rational justification for his conviction.

III. Empirical and Hypothetical Treatment compared.

1. In order then to examine social questions in the past, or to forecast the future, or to see our way about possible improvements, we must enter on a purely empirical investigation; we must lay aside for the present, all postulates about labour and capital, all hypotheses about free competition and formulas of supply and demand. We only require to know the field we are going to examine, and to be very careful about the terms in which we record our investigations. The field of enquiry includes the manner in which human

beings have used the resources at their command to satisfy their needs; in the progress of society these needs have been constantly changing, and the available resources have also changed. But the motive power in these changes has not lain, directly at all events, in the circumstances outside man, but in man himself. He has overcome nature; he has sometimes adapted himself to his environment, or he has more often adapted his environment to himself, and made it more comfortable or more productive. By observing, as carefully as possible, the forces in human nature which have been exerted to satisfy human wants, we shall get a view of the means by which men have maintained themselves, and of the means by which they have, at times, advanced to a new stage of progress. To put the matter in this way is not to neglect the assistance which is given by physical nature in supplying products and forces to man, but it is to take these physical factors into account in the right way; by noting how man's skill enables him to apply them to his needs. The thorough examination of human nature, human skill and human motives, on purely empirical lines would give us, if it could be successfully attempted, the completest account of our complicated society in the present; it would give us too the data by which we might enter on an intelligent comparison with the past, or frame a rational forecast for the future.

2. At the same time, though such empirical investigation is most necessary, especially with a view to historical and social enquiries, it would be an error to suppose that it can enable us to dispense with the methods which have been usually adopted by economists in discussing the industrial and commercial phenomena of the present day. Just because our existing society is so complex, the attempt to proceed empirically would be tedious and could never be complete. By assuming certain conditions which are practically true at present, and neglecting the minor disturbances, we may fix our attention on what is really important here and now. We thus get a convenient method of statement, and that in itself is the first condition for solving a problem.

The volume of commercial transactions in the present day is so great, the machinery by which they are carried on is so complicated and so delicate, that we may welcome any method by which the questions to be considered are simplified. The hypothetical method, which assumes certain facts of human nature, and works on the basis of this assumption, is most convenient for discussing all matters of currency and banking, all questions connected with commerce or tariffs or the Stock Exchange. The empirical enquiry, on the other hand, is the most convenient for dealing with the distant past or the probable future; even if we merely rely on it in order to enable us to correct our hypotheses, and adjust results we have already reached, and restate them so as to apply in other circumstances. There are topics in regard to which there may be much doubt as to which of the two methods is the more convenient; such are questions about labour and wages in the immediate future.

These two modes of treatment, then, are not inconsistent and need not be opposed; but it is desirable to distinguish them, so that we may not flounder helplessly between them, and thus fail to know the precise character of the results we have attained. It is not easy always to distinguish them; they are closely connected, and neither can claim to occupy the whole field of economic enquiry to the exclusion of the other. The empirical enquirer, who would dispense with the assistance of hypotheses, undertakes unnecessary drudgery in intricate paths, in which he may easily lose his way. The economist who betrays any jealousy of the progress of empirical enquiry, as likely to do serious damage to the science, is self-condemned. After all, neither method of enquiry can be pursued entirely apart from the other; we cannot without empirical enquiry reach the facts of human nature and of the physical world which Mill assumes; and the tentative use of hypotheses is an ordinary instrument in any empirical investigation. Still, the two modes of treating economic phenomena, though not mutually exclusive, and though neither supersedes the use of the other, are yet so far distinct that it may be convenient to contrast them as to their general modes of working, and the nature of the results obtained.

3. The hypothetical mode of treatment is conducted on the model which is given by mechanics. Mechanics examines the behaviour of a body moving under its own momentum, and acted on by no force; Economics examines the behaviour of a man actuated by self-interest and uninfluenced by external considerations. The science states how molecules or men regularly act under certain conditions, and thus gives us the law of the phenomena. Economics may then proceed to consider how various kinds of external force interfere with the phenomena and modify the results. To do this, recourse is still had to the methods of Mechanics. A common denominator is taken of the widest kind, so that all the various forces in human nature can be expressed quantitatively in similar terms; some writers prefer to speak of greater or lesser quantities of motive, and some of greater or lesser quantities of the utility which attracts; but they are alike in this, that the whole method of conducting the enquiry is based on Mechanics, and the favourite conceptions which are applied to economic phenomena, such as equilibrium, are borrowed from mechanical science.

(*a*) The advantage of this method, lies in the convenience it offers for carrying on a difficult enquiry about the complicated affairs of the present day; but it is not without defect, so that it may occasionally be supplemented with advantage. It states what holds good upon a given assumption; what is thus formulated is a universal proposition which holds good anywhere and everywhere, so long as the assumed conditions are present. It is valid for all time and for distant planets, and indeed for any possible place that we can ever think about,—because it derives its validity from the very nature of our thinking faculty; given the condition, the consequent is necessary. But although it has this hypothetical validity universally, it may not be actually true in any single place, or at any known time; it will never be true unless the assumed condition is present. On the other hand, though empirical investigation cannot give us economic laws which are valid in other planets, it can help us to learn what is actually occurring in the world where we live.

(*b*) Again, economists who have devoted themselves to hypothetical enquiries find that they can proceed without any detailed analysis of human motives. The various objects of human desire are sufficiently represented for their purpose by greater or less quantities of utility, and we find that they do not lay any stress on the need for analysing different kinds of motive or for using accurate terminology. There is even a disposition not to define the most important terms; it is taken for granted that everybody knows the sort of thing to which they apply, and that no greater precision can be hoped for than is attained in ordinary conversation. Thus we are told in common primers that capital cannot be separated from non-capital by 'a precise dividing line' and that 'productive labour cannot be divided off by a clearly dividing line from unproductive.' But accuracy in the use of terms is of the first importance in an empirical investigation; we must know what a name means, or we cannot advance with a discussion of the things to which it applies. In economics it is indeed comparatively easy to define the names, the difficulty generally lies in the fact that our defective powers of observation may render it hard for us to know at once on which side of our precisely drawn line an imperfectly understood object ought to be placed.

(*c*) In investigating movement within certain conditions it is natural to apply mechanical analogies, as they may give the most convenient method of summarising the facts we wish to explain. Such conceptions as equilibrium or the equation of supply and demand offer convenient modes of exhibiting the influences which determine prices at any one moment on the Stock Exchange, and they can be applied to show the ordinary price of corn which ruled during a long period, like a century. But for the most part they are methods of stating, or it may be of illustrating, economic phenomena, rather than methods of explaining the reasons of the changes which have actually taken place. To apply the conception of equilibrium we must break up the course of events into longer or shorter periods; and if we wish to follow out a continuous change, whether of progress or decay, it is generally more convenient to discard the analogies and conceptions drawn from elementary mechanics; growth and decay and other ideas borrowed from organic life are more likely to serve our purpose and to prove convenient phraseology.

4. Since empirical investigation of economic phenomena discards the assumptions with which Mill and many of the other followers of Adam Smith have started, we must, in pursuing it, forego the convenient aid which we may derive by drawing mechanical analogies, and we must therefore force ourselves to carry out our analysis as fully as may be with the use of ordinary language; and we must be careful to employ our terms with precision. Above all, we cannot hope to attain results which are universally valid, but only statements which are true to the facts of actual life, over a larger or smaller area, and for a longer or shorter period, on the globe we inhabit. In so far as we notice the operation of a motive—like the wish to have a reserve fund —which shows itself in early races, and which is maintained in a highly developed form among civilised men, we may perhaps attain to a statement which is true very widely and which is therefore very important; in other cases we may have to notice the influence of passing whims of fashion.

IV. Respective Advantages of the Two Methods of Study.

It has seemed wise to endeavour to distinguish thus clearly the method which is adopted in most treatises on economic science from that which will be pursued in the following pages. Each is good in its own place. However highly we rate the importance of hypothetical enquiries, we may yet feel that they require to be supplemented by empirical studies. So too, while entering on an empirical investigation, I may once more reiterate my repudiation of the view that this is the only legitimate mode of economic enquiry and that hypothetical statements are foolishness.

By the assumption of free competition we simplify many problems and are able to examine affairs of present importance, which could hardly be discussed at all, unless they were artificially isolated so that we may observe them better; it affords a most valuable means of investigation with which we cannot dispense. It supplies us with terms in which to describe phenomena we observe, and general propositions with which to compare our empirical conclusions. For all that however, by adhering rigidly to this assumption we condemn ourselves to think within a limited range; it ·may be desirable to try and break through this charmed circle if we can. We must certainly do so if we wanted to review the whole industrial life of our own time, to see wherein it differs from that of bygone ages; and how it may be improved; but this would be a very large undertaking. It will more than suffice for the present to take one factor, Capital, and examine it more closely, as it is now, and see how it differs from the corresponding factors in bygone days. When we have examined it thus we shall be able to look at questions connected with the remuneration of capital and the duties of the capitalist in a new light, or at least in light derived from sources that have been too much neglected.

In so far as the attempt to examine modern capital more closely, and to name the personal elements which are concerned with it, is at all successful, in so far we shall get results that are more widely true than the statements of modern economists who have adopted such assumptions as those of Adam Smith or Mill. These statements have of course hypothetical validity of a universal character; but they do not hold good as convenient descriptions of the actual course of industrial affairs, except for a few countries and for these countries in comparatively recent times. They assume free competition and trace everything to the individual desire of wealth-in-general as an ultimate explanation; but there is only a small area of human life on this globe in which the individual 'desire of wealth' has free scope enough to make itself felt as a dominant force. When we

take account of a variety of human motives in the present
day, and note the particular characters of each, we shall find
that some of them are forces which have been effective from
very early times and over wide areas, e. g. the desire not of
wealth-in-general, but of having a hoard. In so far as we
can succeed in tracing out the influence of some very elementary human desire which shows itself in very primitive
races, who have very little knowledge of nature or power of
controlling it, we shall reach an economic principle which
has held good in the most different times and places as an
explanation of actual life there and then.   The desire of
wealth-in-general is a complicated product that shows itself
among men in highly civilised society ; we must look for the
simpler, because more particular, motives which are combined
in it now, and which have operated in earlier social conditions
as well.

CHAPTER II.

Industry without Capital.

I. Money and Capital.

1. A MAN's capital, as we talk about it in the present day, is understood to be a fund of wealth from which he expects to get an income. This is what is meant by the word in ordinary conversation, and it will serve for the present as a definition of the thing. The precise force of the various terms in this phrase will be brought out in subsequent discussion, at present it may suffice to point out that this income will be received in money and pass through the owner's account at the bankers; there is probably no part, or only a very small part, which is paid to him in kind. The fund itself at any time consists of property of different sorts; but it is constantly estimated in terms of money, and this estimate states the amount of money which could be obtained for it at that time. It is ordinarily assumed that a man can realise his capital in money, and subsequently reinvest it in some other property. He may indeed sink it in land; but when he does, common opinion rightly regards him not as a capitalist but as a landlord, for his wealth no longer exists as capital, since it is merged in an estate and cannot be realised apart from that estate (p. 85). The wisdom of the capitalist lies in making judicious investments, in weeding his investments from time to time, or holding an improving property. A man's whole capital will very rarely actually be in the form of money, but it is always potential money; and many judicious capitalists dislike investments in which their

money is so locked up that they may be unable to realise it when they desire to do so. This is one of the reasons why so many private firms have been reconstructed as joint stock companies; the partners can more easily withdraw a portion of the capital, if, e.g. it is necessary to divide the estate among heirs. Hence capital, as we habitually think of it, is a fund of wealth, realisable in money, and from which the owner expects to derive a money income.

2. From all this it follows that capital, as we speak of it to-day, can only exist where money is generally known and used, or, to put it in another way, where the exchange of wealth is regularly practised and men are familiar with the use of a medium of exchange. You may have a hoard of goods, but unless you can employ it in the expectation of income, it is not capital, properly so called. The Bombay rayat, who has a store of corn (beyond what he needs for seed), who cannot sell it, but holds it against a famine year, does not expect to get any income from it; it is a reserve fund rather than capital, it is wealth which is lying idle. If those who merely keep their hoards as a reserve and do not use them are not capitalists, it is still more obvious that those who do not even form hoards at all but merely live from hand to mouth have no capital. In any state of society where everybody lives from hand to mouth there is no capital; a tribe that lives solely by hunting wild animals or fishing, and which has no store on which it can fall back, has no fund of wealth and therefore has no capital.

3. While it thus appears that there are many peoples who have no capital it is also true that there are tribes which continue to live in this hand to mouth fashion, and manage on the whole to obtain supplies, and satisfy their needs from day to day; it is also true that there are many villages which are almost entirely isolated, which do not rely on trade for the supply of any of their regular wants, and which yet maintain themselves in moderate comfort from year to year; they produce all that is necessary for subsistence year after year. They may be very industrious, and practise all sorts of useful arts, but they have not reached the social conditions

which are implied in the very nature of capital.   But if tribes
of hunters, or self-sufficing villages, procure what is needed
to satisfy their wants without capital, it is perfectly obvious
that capital, as we know it, is not a requisite of production
in all times and in all places.   To say that capital is a requisite for production in a capitalistic era is a mere truism ;
and since modern society is capitalistic it is true to say that
capital is a requisite of production in modern society ; but
the fact that capital is necessary for carrying on industry as
it is organised in Europe in modern times does not show
that capital is necessary for production at all times and in
all places.

4. ' But surely,' it may be said, ' industry could not go on
unless there were something similar to capital in these primitive circumstances, something that discharged similar functions.'   Very likely it could not ; we shall be better able to
discuss the matter if we can arrive at a clear view as to the
precise function that capital performs ; in the meantime it
may suffice to point out that a thing may be similar and not
the same ; the very question we want to discuss is just this —
How far are they similar?   If we begin by calling them by
the same name, we are begging the whole question, and assuming that they are so closely similar, that we may use the
same term for both.   Birds fly and bats fly and so do flying
fish and butterflies, we may say that they have all got wings
and leave the matter there ; but there are great differences
between their wings, as birds fly with their arms and bats
with their fingers ; the wings of the others have even less
resemblance to the limb with which the bird flies ; there is
a certain likeness between them all, but when we think for
a moment we see that the resemblance is very slight.   The
use of the word wings suffices for popular talk and for poetry,
but we have to discard it if we wish for scientific accuracy.
It is true that the tribes of hunters possess certain implements, and that agricultural villages have not only implements but a store of food ; but here the likeness to capital
ends.   To call these implements and stores capital may serve
in travellers' tales, but it does not conduce to clearness of

thought and accuracy of language. There is a constant danger of expanding the application of a term by analogy till it loses all definite signification and becomes a mere metaphor. No one would seriously contend that the 'Flying Scotchman' must have wings, or that it goes on 'the wings of the wind'; but economists have sometimes strained analogies, and used words in loose senses until they have fallen into strange absurdities.

5. There is much greater danger of confusion, if we allow ourselves to take liberties with economic terms, than there can be in pursuing any branch of natural science. The distinction between the wing of a bird and that of a bat is clearly marked when once it is recognised; but the implements and stores of a primitive people not only correspond to the capital of modern society, but they may also be said to be undeveloped forms which give rise to capital as it is used in modern industry; they are related, somewhat as the caterpillar and the moth. Capital supersedes the primitive arrangements for industry and takes its place; it does this very gradually. Just because the process is slow and continuous we need to have clear terminology in order that we may be able to discriminate the stages in the process. The caterpillar and the butterfly have one continuous life, but that is no reason for saying that the caterpillar is a butterfly and calling them both by the same name. The industrial life of the English people has been continuous from the time when their separate villages were each practically self-sufficing, but that is no reason for saying that the requisites of production now were the requisites of production then, and calling them by the same names. Both for the sake of understanding the nature of capital, and in order to trace the development of society, we shall do well to avoid the vague use of terms and to try and discriminate the real differences between these early societies and our own.

II. Physical Circumstances and Personal Qualities.

1. There are two distinct points of view from which we may look at the differences between primitive and civilised

society, and therefore two distinct sets of phrases and terms by which we may describe them, or different sets of elements into which we may resolve the forces that work in them. Man and his environment act and react on one another; we may fix our attention on man's physical surroundings, and describe the changes in the material conditions of his life; or we may attend chiefly to man and describe the changes in his powers of overcoming nature and improving his circumstances. We are apt to vary, in a somewhat haphazard fashion, between these modes of statement; sometimes to use one set of phrases and sometimes another, but the state of affairs to be described is always affected by both elements. Travellers who write about the North American Indians and other such tribes are fond of laying stress on their improvidence—a personal quality. They have abundant food one day, but they never attempt to save it, and if they have bad luck they may soon be reduced to the direst straits. But though the improvidence is so noticeable, it may also be said that they hardly have any suitable materials for hoarding; that the flesh on which they live is not easy to preserve, and that the whole physical circumstances of their life make it difficult for them to be very provident.

In regard to agricultural communities we may note something similar; they do not exchange their goods regularly and habitually, and we may say that they have no roads or other means of communication and that physical circumstances are against them. On the other hand it appears that they have no great wish to break down these obstacles and have not enterprise enough to try and open up trade; they would regard it as a doubtful boon.

2. Now though these physical and personal traits appear to be distinct, they are after all very closely related and are separate ways of stating the matter. Certain physical circumstances are a limit to certain men, because they have not the wish or the wit to overcome them—a personal defect; to other men with more personal resources these same physical obstacles cease to be an insuperable barrier. As human skill increases, the old limits which circumstances set to

human welfare are passed; no such physical circumstance can be an absolute bar to further progress, though it is a barrier that is insuperable until human intelligence improves. It may be said that the physical circumstances which prove a barrier in any society show the high water mark of the skill and enterprise of that society. The two are closely related, and in accounting for the low condition of any race we may lay stress either on physical circumstances or on the character of the people—their wishes and habits. We may say that it is impossible for them to do otherwise because of their surroundings, or we may say that it is impossible for them to do otherwise because of their habits and dispositions; the two are correlative.

3. For some purposes one mode of statement is more convenient, for others another. We may notice that for the purpose of describing how great the difference is, we do well to keep to the physical circumstances, because we can note and describe them; but we may make a mistake in speaking positively about inherent disposition and character because these are after all matters of inference. Although the physical conditions are most easily described, it does not follow that they are the most potent factors and that human character is really formed by them; the whole history of civilisation refutes such a supposition; wherever human powers are improved, and men become more skilful or energetic, or self-reliant, or able to co-operate with one another, they are sure to obtain a greater command over nature, and a better means of supplying their wants. And here we may perhaps say that while the material adjuncts of any state of society may often give us the best means of estimating the stage of progress it has reached, the personal elements of skill and character supply an ultimate explanation of any definite progress in the arts of life. It is ultimate so far as economics are concerned, for it takes. us outside the sphere of wealth altogether, and to carry the matter farther we should have to enter on a fresh enquiry and to examine the growth of mind and character.

4. (*a*) By looking at their physical conditions and ap-

pliances we find plain features which distinguish societies of human beings, where there is no capital, from others. They have no means of communication or regular commerce and no sufficient medium of exchange. Unless there is an abundant medium of exchange it is impossible to accumulate a fund of such wealth as can be transferred from one kind of employment to another; there may be hoards of food or other wealth, but these hoards cannot be realised or employed at will in any kind of industry or direction of commerce. It is when there is money, or a circulating medium, that the men who have masses of money, have a fund of wealth which is readily transferable, and thus it appears that habitual commerce and the use of a medium of exchange is a necessary condition, without which the formation of capital cannot take place at all. These are not the sole conditions, for the general accumulation of capital may not take place even though these conditions are present, as the history of mediaeval England shows; but where these phenomena do not appear, capital cannot come into being.

(*b*) The absence of trade is a plain fact, the explanation of the fact is found in the personal characteristics of the people. If we wish not only to call attention to the difference but to ask for the reasons why some races have no regular commerce and medium of exchange, we may note three personal qualities which must all be present before trade becomes habitual. They must (a) be so far on friendly terms with their neighbours that they can meet and drive bargains. (β) They must be able to produce or procure something to exchange, and (γ) they must be able to keep and stow things to exchange. Neighbourliness, Skill, Providence—if any one of these personal qualities is absent, there can be no regular commerce; possibly all three traits may alike be wanting in the case of mere hunters or the most savage races; but if any one were absent, regular commerce could hardly be developed, and travellers ought possibly to be more careful before ascribing the backward condition of any race to some one personal characteristic, as e. g. improvidence; it must be a matter of inference which personal quality is lacking or how far all are weak. It is, however, clear that where these three personal qualities are present in the people of adjacent social groups which have dissimilar productions, commerce is likely to arise; and the more friendly relations, skilful production, and patient foresight are cultivated, the more widely and securely may regular commerce be extended; it is hardly necessary to show that it goes on more easily and advantageously when a medium of exchange is understood, and money dealings have taken the place of barter.

It is not very clear whether it is possible for regular commerce to go on without the use of a circulating medium. It appears that the Dyaks of Borneo are accustomed to barter one thing for another, but cannot grasp the advantages of a three-cornered exchange or the use of a medium. 'A Dyak,' according to Mr. Brooke, 'has no conception of a circulating medium. He may be seen wandering in the bazaar with a ball of beeswax in his hand for days together, because he cannot find any one willing to take it for the exact article he requires. This article may not be more than a tenth of the value of the beeswax, but he would not sell it for money, and then buy what he wants. From the first, he had the particular article in his mind's eye, and worked for the identical ball of beeswax with which and nothing else to purchase it.' There are other cases too, such as the commerce of half-agricultural, half-piratical traders who used slaves as a means of measuring wealth,—where it is not quite clear that these human chattels are properly spoken of as a medium of exchange; their importance chiefly lay in their capacity for labour, and their use as a measure of wealth was secondary. Of the precious metals it may be said that they are, over a large surface of the globe, chiefly used as media of exchange, and that the other employments are subsidiary; at any rate they are media of exchange which can be readily hoarded, as slaves cannot. When skill and intercourse so far advance that men use metallic money, or a kind of money which can be accumulated, then it appears that, as far as physical conditions are concerned, capital may be formed and funds of wealth accumulated and used in the hope of obtaining an income. But where there is no commerce and no money, there may of course be hoards of food or wealth, but there is no opportunity for forming or investing capital.

5. Besides the conditions which are requisite for the formation of hoards of money, there are others which must be present, before the owner can expect an income or be willing to employ his money. Even in societies where there are considerable hoards of money, there may be a comparatively limited field for using them as capital. The man who has a fund of money will not wish to let it out of his keeping unless he sees his way to be a gainer by doing so. He will not wish to employ it in any direction in which he cannot be sure of an income—a return in money. But even when society has made great advances there may be difficulty in procuring this, for neither agricultural nor industrial pursuits will serve his turn so long as they are pursued for the sake of livelihood or convenience, not for sale in a market for profit on the sale. The mediaeval estate in England was managed as an independent group; and a comparatively small proportion of the produce was sold. The bailiff would endeavour to provide seed corn and food for the household, together with supplies for the lord' and his retainers; he would sell any balance he could spare and improve the buildings or condition of the estate with the receipts in good years; he would have proved that the estate was well maintained by showing that the wealth under his charge had not diminished in any separate item; the estate paid its way and prospered. Only when the whole produce was brought to market and turned into money did it become natural to calculate out the relation between the worth of the estate and the annual return; only then too did market considerations come to be dominant, and the owner began to use the land in the way that would pay best—for sheep farming or for growing corn, as the case might be. In the old days he had managed his estate as the source of provision for his household—as an isolated and, so far as might be, self-sufficing whole and sold the surplus he could spare. Not till

landowners managed their estates in such a fashion as to yield the best return, has agriculture assumed a shape in which it can be taken up as a suitable field for the operations of the capitalist.   The change took place when the latifundia superseded the citizen farming of Rome, and reappeared when sheep-farming was substituted for arable cultivation in Tudor England.

Similarly there was a long period in English industry when the artisans were ready to work up the materials which others supplied, and obtained a living by their labour, but they scarcely made money.   They did their work, and took a respectable place in their calling and trained their sons to follow them, but they fingered very little money and they did not grow rich.   One English industry appears to have taken a new form in the fifteenth century; the clothiers were rich men who could buy up the wool and let it out to craftsmen to work up in their cottages, while they received the finished goods and sold them to retailers or exporters; they did not themselves work for a living, but they tried to meet the market, and their operations were profitable or not, according to the prices which ruled in distant marts.   Here too the possibility of turning a profit determined the fashion or materials of the work that was done; the clothiers, by setting men to work, obtained an income for themselves; when this occurred we may say that the staple trade of England had assumed a shape in which capital might be attracted to it.

So long as men pursue their calling with the view of providing for their own wants, or getting a living, and only sell an occasional surplus, they may continue to carry on industry, but they cannot make annual money payments such as the capitalist desires.   It is quite another matter when the produce is all taken to market, and the possibilities of getting a price and making a profit determine the scale and the direction which the industry shall take.   Where any business thus becomes interpenetrated with pecuniary considerations, it assumes a form in which the capitalist may invest in it.   So soon as the prospects of getting a price are the ruling considerations which affect the conditions of production, it is possible for the capitalist to intervene. But when any one carries on an employment as a bye-industry, or works for regular rations allowed by another, or makes goods that he means to use himself, the variations of price in the nearest market for the articles he produces will affect him but little. Hence we need not expect to find, even in countries where capital has been formed very largely, that it is used in all industries alike. Some trades may be carried on by persons who have little or no capital, and work for their living, while others are organised with reference to a regular market, and managed by capitalists. Or we may have the two types side by side in the same employment, as is the case with dressmaking and cooking. A lady's maid and a domestic cook have no capital, but there must be many thousands invested in some large establishments in Regent Street or in such firms of caterers as Spiers and Pond. In England, at the present day, capital has come to be used in connexion with every sort of industrial operation as well as in agriculture and in commerce, and this is therefore pre-eminently a capitalistic era. But it would not be a little interesting to trace the steps by which this has come about and to see how capital has invaded first one field and then another.

There are then two sets of conditions, one having relation to the formation of hoards of money, another to the possibility of using these hoards so as to obtain an income, which must be taken into account. When both are generally present in any society we may say that it has entered on the capitalistic era. On the other hand, there are some societies in which there is no capital at all, because there is no fund of money, and in others the role of capital is very limited, because there are so few employments which provide an income. If a circulating medium is used and the conditions are present which render the formation of capital possible, there can be little doubt that it will be possible to employ it in commerce; the opportunity of applying it to industry and to agriculture will generally follow later when these employments are taken up not merely as means of livelihood, but for the sake of profit.

III.   Gradual Introduction and great Importance of Capital.

1. This fact that capitalist organisation has only been applied gradually and bit by bit to different spheres of commercial and industrial life renders it necessary to call attention to a defeet in the mode which many economists have adopted in treating the subject.   They have taken capital employed in industry as typical: some have dealt with it exclusively and others have regarded it as the ordinary form which deserved primary attention.   But capital may be engaged in commerce, or regularly employed for lending, in lands where it is never used in connexion with agriculture or industry.   The application of capital to commerce is earlier as well as more widely diffused than the application of capital to industry.   Those who fix their attention on a special form of capital may attach undue importance to some accidental feature, and this may affect their treatment of the whole subject.   The functions of capital are less likely to be clearly seen when we confine our attention to a special and later development.

Thus if it be said that capital is wealth used for the production of more wealth, the definition will hold good of all capital applied to industry, but it is not true of all capital as such.   The goldsmiths lent Charles II money to enable him to pay his way till the taxes could be collected, and not at all to enable him to engage in industry and produce more wealth.   It was capital belonging to themselves and their customers from which they hoped to get an income, and the stop of the Exchequer threatened them with ruin by depriving them indefinitely of their capital and their interest.   It is absurd to define capital by mere reference to one of the possible uses to which it may be applied.   Popular language regards the goldsmiths' wealth as capital, even though it was not applied to productive industry, and it is wise to frame a definition so as to include a fund of this kind.

2. The account which has just been given of the conditions which are necessary for the formation of, and the employment of capital may also serve to throw some light on the question

which has been so much debated as to whether capital is an
' historic category' or not; an ' historic category' may be
said to be a conception which is applicable to mundane
phenomena at some stage of progress, but which is not
applicable to them as they have been at all times and in all
places.   There is certain implied argument which has given a
tinge of acerbity to the discussion ; for it seems to be assumed
on both sides that if an economic form has come into
existence, it cannot be a permanent element in our industrial life.   Those who regard capital as a factor of the first
importance in existing industry are disposed to deny that
there could ever have been a time when it did not exist, or a
time when it will cease to be.   Those who regard capital as
the ' enemy ' are inclined to insist that industry was carried
on for centuries without its aid, and therefore to assert that
no serious loss would ensue if it were to disappear as a
separate factor.   Certainly no one who accepts the doctrine
of evolution will deny that capital has come into being
somehow, and is not a part of the eternal nature of things.
In the preceding pages an attempt has been made to indicate the conditions under which it is called into being ;
they are conditions of life and habit which are very widely
diffused, and so long as they subsist, capital is likely enough
to be maintained.   If we fell back upon barter, or if men
broke up society into self-sufficing communities which each
worked for a livelihood and did not trade, capital could not
in all probability long survive.   But it is a powerful factor in
industrial life and progress at present, and is likely enough
to be permanent so long as the conditions survive.

All permanence in phenomena as known to us is only
relative at best ; it is at least conceivable that matter and
its properties are historic categories, and that the material
universe was at one time composed of ether which had not
yet been formed into vortices.   After all, the important thing
is, that matter exists now, and that since matter has been
formed, the movements of the planets take place according
to the law of gravitation.   It is strange if any one is prepared to contend seriously that capital is not an historic

category which has become applicable in the progress of society, and to argue that it is an eternal existence. But the plain fact that capital has come into existence within historic times in no way diminishes its importance in these societies where it does now exist, and gives no reason to suppose that it might be swept away, without injuring industry. The earliest forms of animal life possess neither stomach nor heart, but that does not prove that the stomach and the heart are useless organs in the anthropoid apes, and might be removed without serious damage. But experience goes to show that any society, in which the necessary conditions are present, is better provided with the necessaries and comforts of life, when its members form capital and proceed to apply it to commerce and industry and agriculture as opportunity serves. Capital comes into being in what Adam Smith called the 'natural progress of opulence,' and there need be no expectation of its disappearance unless it can be shown that the natural progress of opulence proceeds better without it.

CHAPTER III.

CAPITALIST ERA.

I. Capitalist Era in England.

1. CAPITAL may be formed in any country where the use of money is familiar and habitual, it may be applied in any direction where commerce or industry are so organised that a money-income may be expected. There have been lands where it was unknown, or where the sphere of investment was small, but we live in a time when it permeates the whole of our economic life. There is no kind of business into which capital may not be drawn, and all the affairs of the day are affected by its influence, as business of every kind is organised on capitalistic lines, and it exercises a considerable amount of political power.

In the fifteenth century the capitalist was just beginning to make his presence felt in connexion with industry, and there were wealthy clothiers. In the present day capital is the dominating power in all kinds of work. This is largely due to the introduction of machinery; in old days a trade prospered if the workmen were skilled, and it could scarcely be transplanted without the migration of men who could practise the art; skilled labour was the most important factor in production. But in our days machinery does the work more accurately and more cheaply than labourers can, and the capitalists who own the machinery have a very superior position in administering any branch of production; the dominant power is theirs.

In agriculture too we have similar phenomena. The old-fashioned idea of living on the land and selling the surplus has completely gone out; the landlord may be a capitalist who purchases an estate as he might buy any other property, in the expectation of making it pay; and the English farmer is generally a capitalist who works for a return in money. It has been a common complaint in recent years that though the crops are good the farmer cannot get a remunerative price, and that he is therefore carrying on his business without any profit. Many of those who have remedies for the depressed state of agriculture are inclined to blame the farmer for not meeting the market better by trying fruit farming or something else than corn growing. Both the complaints and the proposed remedies serve to show how completely the agricultural interest is interpenetrated by capital, and how generally the conditions which Ricardo assumed in his theory of rent, hold true in England at the present time.

2. Capital too supplies the means by which the government of the country—whether national or municipal—is carried on. National borrowing often provides for military and other expenses, and municipal borrowing secures the use of capital for urban improvements. The power of national creditors may sometimes be an element of danger; certainly the hold which English capitalists have upon other countries, and their desire to protect their interests in Egypt or Turkey, may lead to difficult complications. At any rate it is clear that this economic factor interpenetrates the whole of our political life.

Indeed the variety of the directions in which capital plays a part becomes obvious in a moment if we look at the complicated but delicate machinery by which its movements are effected. The whole of the banking system of England, connected as it is with the banking system of the world, is largely engaged in the transfer of capital; the Stock Exchange, with all the vast numbers of shares and securities which are constantly dealt with, shows the immense amount of capital which is available for carrying on business of any kind or engaging in new enterprises.

3. Several of the different remedies which are proposed for
the social difficulties of the time also indirectly serve to illustrate the acknowledged power of capital; philanthropists very
often propose to rectify the wrongs of our times by a more
widely diffused possession of this factor in production. Some
adjure the working classes to be thrifty by means of Post
Office Savings Banks; some advocate the co-operative
societies, where the consumers of goods become partners
in a business for supplying one another; others suggest
that shares in the capital of a business should be assigned to
the employés so that they may honestly be sharers in the
profits. But all these remedies are expedients for inducing
the artisan to exercise capitalistic virtues and thus to become
a sharer in capitalistic gains.

Since capital is so dominant in industry and agriculture
as well as in commerce, in politics and social reform, it
seems to deserve very special study. There is no other
influence in our day that is so all pervading, there is no other
economic factor that is so powerful, whether for good or for
evil. It is the very life-blood of our existing civilisation, and
hence the attacks of those who wish to see this ended are
concentrated on capital; while those who hope for the
modification and improvement of our present society are
bound to look closely for defects in this quarter. More than
this, the dominance of capital over other interests is a comparatively new thing in our land, and it is not unreasonable
to hope that we shall at least get clearer light on the problems that are new and pressing in the present day when we
concentrate attention on this special feature. But though
comparatively new in the history of our race it is not new in
the world. There has at any rate once before been a time
when capital was all pervading, and its influence strikingly
felt—not in building up the greatness of England, but in laying
the foundations of the Empire of Rome. From the time of
the Punic Wars the sinews of Roman strength were not supplied by the valour of peasant citizens, but by the enterprise of
wealthy capitalists; it was through their organisation and
resource that the Roman Republic became mistress of the

world. In the failure of the Equites to maintain a leading position under the Empire there was a final judgment upon their failure as administrators, and the rule which they had done so much to build up finally succumbed because of weakness which was inherent in their policy from the first.

II. Capitalist Era in Rome.

1. In Republican Rome, as in England to-day, there was a very wide field for the investment of capital. One of the earliest opportunities for employing it was found in a system copied from Greeks and Orientals. This consisted in farming out the taxes, a mode of collection which is always apt to be extortionate, as there can be no proper check on the rapacity of minor officials. Great companies with shareholders (*socius, particeps*) in Rome and factors (*negociatores*) in the Provinces undertook the collection of the customs or of the tithe; but they were also engaged in industrial as well as fiscal undertakings. In the province of Asia—one of the few provinces which not only paid the internal expenses but yielded a large money income to Rome—there were great gangs of slaves owned by Roman capitalists, and engaged in the salt pits or in agriculture. Mining enterprise was carried on in the same fashion; while the importation of corn for largesses, the equipment of the armies, and the construction of public works, all gave scope for the operations of contractors. The whole business of state was let out to capitalists, and these capitalists were organised in companies consisting of many shareholders, some of whom had large holdings (*partes*), while others had but small investments (*particulae*). The forum and the basilicas were the chief haunts of these capitalists, and the shares in the different undertakings were capable of transfer. The conquests of Rome were made by armies fitted out by Roman capitalists; the provinces of Rome were administered and their resources developed by Roman capitalists; the city of Rome was embellished, and the populace of Rome was amused and fed, by

the enterprise of Roman capitalists. Affairs of every kind were carried on by contractors, who manipulated the money of the inhabitants of Rome and other towns, and executed the work by means of armies of slaves.

2. There are some not unimportant differences in the manner in which business was conducted by Roman and by modern capitalists; their relations to the State were somewhat different, as the usual form in Rome was that of contracting for a particular piece of work, not that of lending money to the State to be administered by its own officials. The London capitalist invests his money in the funds or in some municipal loan; the Roman capitalist formed a company to contract for some undertaking, as is done by gas and water companies. The national debt has been chiefly raised on the credit of the nation, and not, as in its earliest stages, on the security of particular rights assigned to the lenders. It was only in rare cases that Roman bankers would part with their money on such terms; and there was unusual liberality in the conduct of the bankers who, without security, lent money for the equipment of forces against Hannibal after the battle of Cannae (B. C. 242) on being promised indemnity from the risks of war and of tempest, and on the understanding that they should be paid out of the first money that came into the treasury. The credit system, altogether, was much less developed, and the forms of credit did not supply a circulating medium; there were differences in the forms under which companies were organised and in the relations of the different classes of members, but on the whole the two social conditions present interesting analogies, because of the dominance of capital in both cases.

3. Capital was a political power in the Roman Republic, however, in a sense in which it has never yet been in England. There are some similarities, for commercial jealousy led to the destruction of Carthage and Corinth—the two rival mercantile powers,—and we have ample analogies to these struggles in the history of our conflicts with Holland and with France. But, in the extraordinary power of the monied men in the State, Rome stands alone; their unexam-

pled influence was the effect of the legislation of the Gracchi, who desired to raise a counterbalancing influence to the patricians. The *equites*, or monied men, thus acquired judicial power; while the small shareholders whom they influenced were so numerous that they also controlled the legislative power in the *comitia*. The distributions of corn which began at the time of the Gracchi rendered tillage unprofitable near Rome, and opened up a field for the profitable employment of capital in pasture farming in Italy, and in the importation of foreign corn. Capitalists had replaced citizen farmers in the land, they controlled the food supply of Rome, and they were the agents by which the military system and provincial governments were administered. They had vast economic powers, and they were to a large extent irresponsible in the way they exercised them, till the empire diminished their overweening influence; for they administered the law as judges, and they could control the legislation through the voting power of the members of joint stock companies.

The closest analogy which we have to the Roman system is in the story of the East India Company; but that company was after all closely and jealously watched by an English parliament and public, many of whom had no interest in the great monopoly, and who maintained a jealous criticism of its character. Whatever abuses may have been perpetrated by those who shook the pagoda tree, they were abuses of the system, not parts of the system; the good government of the people of India has been kept in view, with whatever failures and whatever ignorance, throughout the whole period of the company's political dominion; and the friendly relations of many leading men with natives have no parallel in the story of Roman governors or publicans and provincials. Roman dependencies were administered by joint stock companies, the judges were drawn from the leading financiers, the laws were passed by the shareholders; it was as though the whole affairs of government were handed over to the men of Capel Court or of Wall Street, to be carried on according to their own traditions.

Stock Exchange morality in England is said to be low; at

Rome it was lower still. When during the second Punic war the contractors, who had an indemnity for risks at sea, sunk the ships which were taking supplies to the Roman army and obtained large profits by the transaction, the whole power of the financial interest was employed, and at first successfully, to shield them from any punishment for a notorious crime. If this were feasible in regard to a fraud which was perpetrated in regard to the most pressing interests of the Roman people, we may fancy how little control was exercised over those who administered distant provinces or trafficked with half civilised peoples. The Verrine orations show what it was possible for Roman greed to accomplish even in a province which had special constitutional privileges, and how utterly that fertile province had been exhausted. But there is something more instructive in the story of a man like Lucullus, who had set himself to repress unjust exactions in Asia; he earned the dislike of the Roman capitalists and their eloquent spokesmen, and his public career was destroyed. It is scarcely an exaggeration to say that Lucullus was disgraced because he had not done the things of which Warren Hastings and Impey were accused. Under these circumstances it is perhaps strange, not that the provinces suffered so much under these administrators, as that they did not suffer more. But assuredly the picture is black enough; on one hand we find traces of grinding tyranny, on the other there are pictures of horrible outbreaks against the oppressors. Such were the massacres at Cipta (b. c. 112), at Genabum, or the still more terrible risings in Asia, where thousands of Italian merchants were destroyed. When Rome recovered from the financial crisis which ensued, she set herself to redeem these losses, and the overthrow of Jugurtha and of Mithridates, gave her still wider provinces to drain.

4. With the rise of the Imperial power, the capitalistic power which had been concentrated at Rome became somewhat more diffused in different parts of the Empire. The development of equitable jurisdiction, and the strength of the military despotism, reduced the importance of the monied

interest in the State, and diminished the worst abuses which had flourished under its régime. For us, however, the period from the Gracchi to the fall of the Republic is of great interest, as it furnishes instructive analogies, and contrasts with the capitalistic era in which we live.

CHAPTER IV.

MATERIAL PROGRESS AND MORAL INDIFFERENCE.

I. Material Progress and Increased Opportunities.

1. THE facts that capital is so dominant now and was so dominant under the Roman Republic are sufficient to bring into clear relief its extraordinary power. The conquest of the world, the great aqueducts and roads, the very ruins that remain, demonstrate the vast industrial forces which Roman capitalists were able to bring into operation ; it was with their help that the city was transformed and raised from its humble estate as the mere centre of a little district to become the mistress of the world. In similar fashion England has been transformed since the opportunity for the general accumulation and investment of capital began. Since Tudor times there has been an expansion of England far greater than the expansion of Roman power in the last centuries of the Republic. Our command over machinery has effected a revolution in industry of every kind of which they could not dream, and our commerce gives us the means of procuring commodities from lands they never heard of. It has all come about under a capitalistic régime and with the assistance of capital, and though we may for the present defer the enquiry 'Wherein does thy great strength lie?' we are warranted in assuming that capital either possesses or sets free immense industrial energy.

This is still more noticeable if we look at the changes which are being promoted in new countries in the present day. There is a general cry that they require capital in order that their resources may be developed, and the country may be opened up. They are inclined to borrow capital, often rather recklessly, so as to make harbours and railways, and bring as large an area of the territory as possible within the range of international commerce. The power of capital is obvious in the past, and it is recognised in the present as a primary factor without which the progress of even the most fertile country must be indefinitely delayed.

Perhaps however we may ask the questions, Why should these resources be opened up? Why should progress not be delayed? There are optimists who are continually rejoicing over the rapidity of progress; and those who feel that material progress is a good thing can hardly entertain a doubt that the faster the progress goes on the better it is. But there are also pessimists among us who are oppressed by a sense of the numbers of the population, and who fear that it is increasing with leaps and bounds so as to strain the food-producing power of the globe. It may be true that material progress is a good thing, and that the more rapidly it takes place the better; but it is also true that material progress gives opportunities for the increase of population, and that rapid progress gives opportunities for rapid increase. This fact may make it worth while to consider the question whether there is not another side to the shield.

2. What do we mean by material progress? It surely is a greater command over nature, an increase of our skill and enterprise which enables us to make use of things that were hitherto denied us. We pass the old limits. But at present it is usual for human beings to utilise their increased power over nature by securing more sustenance, and to increase in numbers as the limits are removed by the march of progress. It is perfectly clear that every step in progress makes room for an increase of population; and it is also true that somewhere there is an absolute limit to the possible production of food, and that the earth is physically incapable of supporting more than a given number of millions of inhabitants—whatever their skill might be. There is, somewhere or other, an absolute limit to the possible production of the globe, and it

may be guessed that if the present numbers were quadrupled we should be nearing the absolute limit of the possible population. Every step in material progress brings us nearer the absolute limit of possible production, and the more rapidly we advance the sooner we shall reach that absolute limit.

Perhaps it might be well if we went more slowly; if progress were more gradual there would be room for a change in the standard of human comfort, and the margin which invention offered might be used for increasing the well-being of those who now exist rather than in increasing their numbers.

3. But this is an idle dream; and when we look more closely at the conditions which brought about material progress we need not despair. There is no evidence that the mere increase of numbers has lowered the standard of comfort, though there is ample evidence that any population, with a given standard of comfort, will soon people up to the margin marked by any new step in progress. The pressure of population could never alter the limit; skill and enterprise alter the limit and then population fills up the gap that is left. In an age of rapid material progress, population may be expected to increase—not because of any inherent and necessary force, but because material progress has given it room to expand. There have been long periods when there was little material progress, and when, so far as can be seen, there was no serious ‘ pressure of population ’ and no lowering of the standard of comfort. In the present day population increases fast because material progress goes on so fast; but we are not forced to conclude that if progress were checked, the pressure of population would go on remorselessly and become increasingly severe. Each step of progress leads us nearer an absolutely stationary state, which is indefinitely distant. It is not quite easy to see why this should be a matter for great self-gratulation, but it is at least a goal which we may contemplate without serious foreboding.

4. Indeed, material progress is a good thing, and we are not justified in setting ourselves to delay it, even if we are alarmed by some of its accompaniments. It is easy to

inveigh against luxury and the evils of misspent wealth, and no one would deny that wealth, like other good things, may be misused; but for all that, wealth is a good thing, and chiefly good on this account,—that it gives the opportunity for making the most of human faculties and powers. The ordinary man who is engaged in drudgery all the day long has no vigour left to devote himself to intellectual pursuits; the woman who is eaten up with anxiety as to the next day's dinner or the next quarter's rent has no heart to cultivate artistic tastes. A genius here and there may rise above these depressing conditions, and though he may be a stronger man because he has risen, he may also be a harder man because he has had to go through so much. The hero is the man who rises despite his surroundings, and there will always be scope for heroic virtue; but the good man is called to make the most of his opportunities, and the greater his opportunities the fuller and richer may his personal life become. The man with many opportunities who makes the most of them is not more meritorious than the man with few opportunities who makes the most of them; but though not a more meritorious man he is in many ways a better man,— more richly endowed and more highly cultivated.

In a very poor community—say a new colony—there can be very little time and very few facilities for mental cultivation, and the opportunities of attaining a high degree of personal development are wanting; those who wish for such opportunities are forced to seek them by visiting, at whatever cost, an old country. In a savage tribe the possibilities are still more remote. Every advance in material wealth in the community will give greater opportunities to the individuals who compose it.

This becomes clear if we contrast the England of the present day with England four hundred years ago. Now there are plenty of books available at low prices, or in free libraries; then there were but few, and these so inaccessible that many men had never the opportunity of reading, and felt no privation in not possessing the power. Again, there are now opportunities for travel, with all its effects in enlarging the mind, which were absolutely wanting then. In old days comparatively few people journeyed far from their birthplace, but now few of the artisans of our midland towns have never seen the sea; and a very large number of rustic folk have paid one visit to London. On the other hand, while gardening was almost unknown in the fifteenth century, the Londoner has now a constant opportunity of seeing the most beautiful flowers of all lands. Cheap printing and cheap travelling have opened up new worlds of interest and thought to the whole population, and thus the great material progress of those four centuries has given the opportunity for great intellectual progress too.

Wealth which is used as a means of increasing mental power or of cultivating artistic refinement is not wasted; and even when it is so used without conscious regard for others, it is not always without a beneficial influence upon the lot of others. Two centuries ago the country squire lived a narrow and coarse life; the elevation in the tone and cultivation of the gentry has given a new direction to the aspirations of the simple. His attempts at imitation do not end in his being as drunk as a lord; and a real effort is being made that the poor should be able to enjoy in public gardens, in museums, in libraries or in clubs, those opportunities of intellectual and artistic improvement which the rich possess in their own homes. It is private wealth which gives these opportunities to the rich, and it is only where the material wealth of the community is large that such opportunities can be afforded to the poor.

5. It is easy to disparage material wealth, to insist that many poor people are more meritorious than many of the rich, to scoff at misused wealth, and to urge that it is a far nobler thing to be virtuous and poor, rather than rich and vicious. Of this it need only be said that it is always wrong to misuse opportunities; that great riches give great opportunities, and that from those to whom much has been given much will be required. Each class in society is too ready to criticise the manner in which others misuse their opportunities; the artisan may misuse the opportunities

given by higher wages and shorter hours, but for all that they are good things, and things he will learn to use. There is no question as to the wickedness of those who misuse wealth, or the fact that many do misuse it. Still it remains true, that wealth may be well used and does afford great opportunities of improving human tastes and powers.

And since wealth may be well used, the pursuit of wealth is not necessarily an evil. It just depends. It is an evil if wealth is pursued for its own sake, and without any care as to how it shall be used; it is not an evil if it is pursued as a means to nobler ends. It is not wrong to be rich, though it is always wrong to be selfish and covetous, whether this selfishness takes the form of amassing wealth like a miser, or of coveting the goods of others like a thief. Money is a power for good that we need not despise, though we would do well to remember that the love of money as such, and for its own sake, is the root of evil. In the case of individuals wealth is often pursued selfishly and greedily for its own sake ;—though the ' money-grubbing' of those who desire to give their children a better education and position than they themselves possessed is humanised and redeemed from much of its baseness. But in the progress of a community as a whole even the wealth amassed by the self-seeking of individuals is sometimes merged indirectly and ultimately in a general gain, and the effects of wealth in providing more general opportunities for personal cultivation are very notable. Material wealth is a good thing in so far as it provides material conditions for improving the intellect and tastes of man.

6. There is, however, an element of truth in the disparagement of wealth, to which it is most important to direct attention. It has been said above (p. 21) that it is not in material surroundings, but in personal elements of skill and character, that the ultimate reason of any step in progress lies. And hence it is true that though favourable material conditions are most important, as without them a high condition of culture cannot be diffused or maintained, they are passive and need to be used by man, for in themselves

they are powerless to produce an elevating influence. That can only come from a personal power that cherishes a higher ideal than is given in its surroundings, and sets itself to actualise that ideal in bettering its surroundings. The poet or the artist or the saint who maintains a purer ideal of life, inspires men to try and live for something better, and thus to take advantage of the opportunities afforded by material wealth. The most worthy ideal is that which holds up the noblest conception of life, one that is never superseded, and yet a conception which can be used as a guiding motive for life. It is in this fashion that the Christian conception of the Kingdom of God upon earth has been such a power in the progress of civilisation. And he who tampers with his ideal, or deliberately sacrifices it, is to be blamed as a renegade, because he has been content to enjoy an easy lot instead of seeking to be true to the best that was in him, so as to teach others to make a better use of the opportunities they possess, whatever they are. Spiritual power, which recognises the divine ideal for man in fullest measure and maintains it, is an active principle, by which material goods may be turned to the best account. And since in the individual human being there is a conflict between the flesh and the spirit, between present comfort and aspiration after a purer, worthier life, there is a truth in the asceticism which would keep the body in subjection, and maintain complete self-mastery lest the love of an ideal nature or of a supernatural Being should be dimmed and decay.

The artist who contemns vulgar excess, and the ascetic who despises mere material comfort for himself, who cultivates the highest aspirations in himself and seeks to rouse them in others, are after all the chief active elements in human progress. They cultivate power of will, moral power, spiritual power. Hence are drawn ideals, in the pursuit of which ordinary men may most fitly use their possessions; but these must remain mere ideals unless there are material conditions which render it possible to actualise them, for others to enjoy as well. Enthusiasts have the moral energy, and they give the stimulus which makes other men long to rise; but though the noblest men may discipline themselves to be independent of wealth and of various comforts, and may thus cultivate moral power of their own, it yet remains true that it is wrong to despise worldly goods with the cynic, and foolish to ignore the external means for good which material wealth supplies, and the opportunities for intellectual and artistic self-development which it affords. The moral power is obtained not by avoiding external goods but by victory over self; and a forced privation of any material good gives no moral power; it may but strengthen the force of passions and desires. It is well to practise self-discipline, but it is also well to remember that all the material things that God has created and made are good if men will use them aright, and that we dare not be wiser than He, or seek to restrain the children of men from enjoying the earth which He has given them, with all that it affords.

7. It is well that opportunities of cultivation should be as widely available as possible, and therefore it is well that the material progress of backward countries should be rapid; it is also desirable that every member of a community should have the largest opportunities for personal self-cultivation; subject only to this one condition,—that care shall be taken that these opportunities shall not be diminished for posterity. This is the motive of a good father in providing for his family; and it ought to be borne in mind by a well organised community. But the largest opportunities, present and future, involve a maintenance and increase of material wealth, and we shall be unwise if we endeavour to enjoy the opportunities of the present without a due regard to providing greater opportunities, and therefore greater material wealth, in the future.

Hence, while advocating the largest diffusion of opportunities, I feel much hesitation about the wisdom of the demand for ' equal opportunities.' Equal opportunities appear to imply equality of material wealth; but this would be futile without a further guarantee of equal capacity for taking advantage of these opportunities. To take the simplest case; the first few years of a child's life are of the highest importance for its future, but some have good homes and some have bad; there can be no real equality of opportunity unless there is similarity in homes; unless, indeed, all be reduced to equality in a foundling hospital. Those who have the worst homes would be benefited, but all who might have had it would lose the advantage of a mother's care and of family life.   Such equality of opportunity could only be obtained by cutting down, and depriving some of the best conditions for well-being, without thereby improving the lot of the others.   We want to give larger opportunities by levelling up, and we ought to want to do it without cutting down.   The man who inveighs against millionaires, and desires that they should be treated as public enemies to be pillaged, is only giving utterance to a greedy, envious spirit, which is ready to cut down the opportunities of some in the present, without considering the danger of sacrificing the possibility of larger opportunities for all in the future.

Progress in the past has not taken place all along the line at once; those that believe that the advance in the future would be better and faster if all ranks of society kept step, as it were, are bound to show a reason for their belief.   There has been an individual use of opportunity here and there, which has kindled similar tastes, until the whole of society has been leavened; the world is richer for the art-patronage of the trading companies of Florence; and the musical enthusiasm of some of the wealthy in this country has given rise to progress in that art by which our whole generation is the better.   Material progress is a good thing when it is used for such ends; it is worth seeking because it gives a greater possibility of striving for such ends.

II. Moral Indifference and its Dangers.

If it be admitted that material progress is a good thing it seems to follow by implication that what contributes to such progress is also good.   There can be no question but that in recent material progress capital has been a very great power, but it is also true that it is a dangerous power, if it is not properly controlled. The story of its action under the Roman Republic is a sufficient illustration of this statement, but it may be worth while to insist on it at some length.

1. The capitalist's chief thought is for the security of the fund he possesses, and his next will be for as large an income as may be; these are the points that come before him in investing his capital. His attention is concentrated on the precise bargain he is making, and the indirect effects of that bargain are so distant and uncertain that he leaves them out of account, and is ordinarily quite indifferent to them.

Thus the capitalist is quite indifferent to political considerations in his management of his money. He may be prepared to join in an outcry against the manufacturer who sends improved patterns of guns to a rival power—say to Russia. But he would feel no scruple in lending his capital to Russia, and thus giving that rival power the means of purchasing the improved arms. There is no great difference between the cases, but he is blind to the possible results of his own action, and thus is indifferent politically.

Again, the capitalist is indifferent to artistic considerations; the craftsman may have an honest pride in his work and dislike sending out goods that he feels are not worthy of him; but if there is a public demand for inferior goods, and capital finds that they pay, it will not scruple to cater for a debased taste and take the profit that accrues.

In similar fashion it may be said that capital is indifferent to the moral and spiritual welfare of those who are employed; it is clear that the directors of joint-stock companies are not legally warranted in spending the property of the shareholders in building churches or schools. And again, capital as capital is indifferent to the manner in which land is employed so long as it yields a return. The old-fashioned landlord may have an attachment for his retainers, but the mere speculator is indifferent whether the land produces corn, or sheep, or deer, so long as the investment pays.

2. Yet, after all, these matters, patriotism and good work-

manship, and culture, are well worth attention; to say that
capital is indifferent to them seems like bringing a charge
against the owners of capital. But it is not said that they
are reckless, only that they are indifferent; it is not contended
that the power of capital is misused, only that it may be
abused by mere neglect. There have indeed been times
when capitalists were not only indifferent but reckless, were
willing to make a profit out of national disaster, and ready to
grind the lives out of unhappy slaves. There is no need to
quicken the sense of danger by hunting for cases of similar
recklessness now; it is surely clear that if the higher aims of
life are habitually left out of account, there is real danger we
shall suffer. That they are habitually left out of account can
hardly be questioned; but before we set ourselves to denounce
capitalists for this neglect, two points have to be considered,
—how far the neglect is really criminal? and next, how far the
individual capitalist is responsible and therefore to blame?

3. Much moral indignation has been expended by socialists
and others on the indifference of capitalists; and demonstra-
tions are commonly current that conduct in regard to economic matters must be judged by standards of right and wrong.
But this no capitalist, however 'hardened,' would ever deny;
some conduct in connexion with the investment of money is
criminal and some is dishonourable, it has an ethical character
plainly enough, and there is severe punishment for fraud. The
difficulty is this,—supposing the transaction is above-board
and public and fair as between man and man, the conscience
of the capitalist is satisfied, and he does not usually feel
bound to inquire into the indirect and remote and ulterior
effects of the transaction. He does not deny that his conduct must be judged by an ethical standard; but so long as
it is a fair and open transaction, he feels that he is not called
upon to indulge in any further subtleties.

There is a parallel which easily presents itself; no one
would deny that there is a right and wrong about matters
of food, but the ordinary conscience is satisfied if its owner is
neither greedy nor a glutton. The plain man who means
well does not feel called upon to inquire too closely as to the

qualities of different foods and their bearing on disposition and character? how far he will be a more intelligent man if he eats fish, or a less passionate man if he abstains from meat? These seem to the ordinary man to be over-refinements, and to show a sensitiveness which is unhealthy and morbid. In much the same way the want of patriotism in which the capitalist may be involved by subscribing to a Russian loan is indirect and uncertain; it seems to be a piece of hyper-sensitiveness to take it into account. And such neglect, though it may be disastrous, is hardly criminal; the man honestly feels that he has acted fairly in the matter himself, and in the bargain he made about transferring the money, and that he is not to be held responsible for the use to which other people put it; the extent of his blameworthiness depends on his means of knowing, and · the reasons for believing, that a hostile use could be made of it.

There are cases, however, where wrong arises directly and immediately in connexion with the administration of capital. A certain company earns large profits and deals oppressively by its hands; the shareholder secures the profits, say twelve per cent., and his capital doubles or trebles in value because of the success of the enterprise. But if this business is oppressively managed, is he not to blame for receiving 'blood-money'? In regard to this too, many honest-minded individuals will feel no scruple, because they have not the time or knowledge to understand the details of the management; each man feels that his own personal share is small, and that he must leave these matters to others. He believes perhaps that newspaper criticism is more effective than the utterances of a single shareholder at a big meeting; his personal part in the administration is practically nil, and he consequently feels no responsibility.

Even in the case of a man who is sole manager of the business in which his capital is invested; he may be a sweater, and know that he is; at the same time he may think, and it may be true, that the public demand for cheapness is such, and the competition of other sweaters is so keen, that his margin of profit is very small, and that any attempt to re-arrange the system on which his business is conducted would do no good to the employées, and would certainly effect his own ruin. He is hemmed in by a crowd of circumstances which keep him from exercising any real responsibility as a matter of fact. He may regret the state of affairs, but he feels that he cannot help it.

It thus appears that the enormous power of capital, which may work so much mischief, if it is not properly controlled, is very imperfectly controlled indeed. Some owners feel no responsibility for distant and indirect results, though these may be of fatal importance ; some feel unable to exercise any real influence on affairs that come under their own cognisance and pass through their own hands. It seems under these circumstances necessary for us to consider the different fashions in which capital is actually administered and controlled in the present day.

CHAPTER V.

THE CONTROL OF CAPITAL.

I. The Different Modes of Administering Capital for Different Objects.

IT might at first sight seem that the control of capital, like the control of other property, would rest entirely with the owners of capital,—subject of course to such general rules about fair dealing as any government felt it necessary to enforce. But the difficulties to which attention was called in the last chapter serve to show that the owners of capital are not always as a matter of fact able to exercise a complete control over the manner in which it is used. Capital is sometimes lent to other persons to use, and then the borrower, not the lender, has the chief voice in directing it; or the force of circumstances may prevent a man from administering it in the fashion he would personally prefer. It may be convenient to look at the matter from another side, and to see how one mode of managing capital or another may be more suitable, according to the purposes for which it is used.

Capital is, as we have seen, a very vigorous factor in promoting material progress; we may try to note a few of the chief elements in material progress, and may enumerate them in order according as they concern the nation as a whole, or larger or similar bodies of citizens. We may thus see how the capital that is devoted to attaining one or other of these several aims is actually administered. For this purpose we may neglect the distinction between borrowed capital and capital that is owned by the man who carries on the business in which it is employed—a distinction which comes to be of

primary importance when we have to consider the remuneration of capital.

1. Certain elements which are requisite for material progress are common to the whole nation; they are facilities
which conduce to progress generally. Though some individuals may feel the importance of them more than others, it
is impossible to say that anyone derives no advantage from
them; but the benefit can hardly be assessed, as it accrues
for the most part in the way of preventing mischief, and not
by furnishing positive gain. The advantage of living in a
civilised community where there is security for life and for
the enjoyment of possessions is obvious; and for commercial
purposes it is also most important that merchants should be
able to reside and to prosecute their calling in distant lands.
In order to procure these conditions, which are so intimately
connected with material progress, there must be (*a*) good judicial administration, (*b*) security from rebellion, war, and even,
if possible, from the fear of war, and (*c*) effective agreements
with distant powers. Now the two first of these conditions
are most likely to be secured when people are self-governed,
or governed by men of their own race, and the last is most
likely to be secured in the case of a great nation which has
a high reputation for power. It thus comes about that loyalty
to the national government, or *Patriotism*, and care for the
national reputation, or *Prestige*, are well worth keeping in
view as underlying conditions which make for material progress. The depression of Greece, Carthage, and Spain when
they fell under Roman rule, of Granada, Portugal, and Flan-
ders under Spanish rule, are cases which seem to show that
the loss of national self-government may exercise a very
malign influence on national industry and commerce. Hence
it comes about that despite the terrible cost of war, and the
loss of life and dislocation of industry and trade which it
involves, it may be expedient to have recourse to war, rather
than lose that national independence or prestige which are
such important conditions for material progress.

Into the moral questions connected with war it is not necessary to enter here; it is enough to say that in so far as mate-

rial progress gives conditions which render a better culture possible, it is difficult to condemn absolutely any step that leads to real material progress and thus to the possibility of further moral advance. War that is unsuccessful has no material justification; it exhausts the country without any real return, and the moral justification of such war is harder to find. It may give a stimulating example of courage and bravery which is a possession for all time; it may be a monument of the folly and foolhardiness of some statesman. Even if a war accomplishes its object, it may be at a cost which proves that it was a curse to the country. The Scottish war of Independence was successful; Wallace and Bruce have left inspiring memories; but it sapped the one constitutional power that was able to control a turbulent nobility, and checked the development of the country till the time when its fatal successes were undone. Such considerations seem to imply that war is a desperate remedy, that the greatest caution should be exercised before a nation has recourse to it; but they do not show that it is never necessary. Without entering on the disputed question as to whether the Napoleonic wars were forced upon us or not, and fully recognising their exhausting effects and the pressure of the burden of debt they have caused, it may yet be contended that it was worth while—according to the terms in which such things can be assessed—for Englishmen to pay largely for the continued power of self-government, and the material prosperity which they have enjoyed through their patriotism and the prestige they acquired.

(*d*) With reference to the national life as a whole, it may be said that there are certain ideal aims which yet react so closely upon material progress that they must be taken into account; in so far as capital is required to carry out operations that are expedient for the sake of patriotism or of prestige, that capital is employed for an object that is common to the whole nation, and may be most fitly administered by the government of the country. What concerns all is the business of all. In the same way it may be contended that intelligence and skill are a benefit to the whole community, and a benefit which is directly exhibited, even if it cannot be accurately expressed, in terms of material wealth. The nation may be concerned both in promoting the advance of know-ledge and research and encouraging discovery; it may also concern itself in seeing that the citizens partake in the know-ledge which is brought within their reach, and expend money on education. In all such matters there may be need for the use of capital, and, when this is called for, it is most naturally administered by public and national authority, since all are concerned in its results. The nation, as a whole, is concerned in these matters, and not any one locality only; and there-fore the administration of capital, so far as it is required for the defence of the nation, the administration of justice, the promotion of the intelligence and character of the inhabitants, is naturally entrusted to the power which has the widest sway within the land, and which determines our relations with other powers. In some cases the maintenance of internal communications with different parts of the realm might be regarded as an object which distinctly concerned the realm as a whole, and should be undertaken by the community as a whole. But it is at least arguable that the maintenance of communications involves minute care and supervision in many districts of the country which are long distances apart, and that this work can be best done, not as a centralised un-dertaking, but by the separate action of district authorities who have the requisite local knowledge. It seems obvious that where certain things have to be done, but can be best done under local supervision, it is simplest for the central authority to work through the local powers and subsidise them; or at any rate to lay down instructions as to certain conditions which it is necessary, in the interest of the whole state, for each separate district to observe. For the present purpose we may be satisfied to insist on the fact that there are separate spheres for national and local government, for State and for municipal authority, without attempting to define these spheres.

2. There are, however, many conditions for material pro-gress which can be best attended to by local authorities such

as municipalities, not by the State. Such, for example, are matters connected with the health of the inhabitants ; this is clearly a prime requisite for material progress, but the conditions which militate against it, or are required to promote it, differ according to the physical character and even the occupations of different localities. The best means of water supply, the best methods of drainage, are obviously problems which take a different form in different places. The deleterious effects of certain gases are felt in the neighbourhood of chemical works, and smoke is a nuisance of different degrees of intensity in different towns, and therefore they may require different modes of regulation in separate cases. Similarly, provision for public recreation, the formation of parks and local museums and galleries, above all of baths, may all be regarded as contributory to physical and moral health, but as matters which are best attended to by municipal rather than State authority.

It may also be the case that the machinery for technical education—unlike that of general education—may be most fitly provided for by local authority. The technical requirements of Leeds, with its textile trades, are very different from those of Sheffield or of Stoke. And if these functions fall within the purview of local authority the municipality will be naturally charged with the duty of administering the capital that is employed in the effort to promote them.

3. There is however in this country a strong feeling that Government management and municipal management are often extravagant, and that in the carrying on of ordinary business operations, the supply of material wants of all sorts, private undertakings are greatly superior. We frequently hear of the cost that is involved in Government dockyards, and municipal gasworks give rise to frequent complaints. It certainly appears that in those cases where careful attention to minute details is specially necessary, the work can be best done by a private individual administering the affair himself. Market gardening may be taken as a case in point; the supply of fresh fruit and vegetables is not a business which the London County Council would be likely to manage better

than the gardeners who send their produce to Covent Garden.
It is one of the arts where there is comparatively little scope
for the introduction of machinery, and where skilful labour
and attention are the main elements of success. In such
cases it may be contended that the capital required for carrying on the business will be best administered by a man who
is on the spot and keenly interested in turning it to account,
that is to say, by a private individual who has the capital
under his own control.   Just as there is a sphere where state-
administration seems best, so there appears to be a sphere
where personal and individual administration is to be preferred.

4. Besides the enterprises where individual management is
apparently preferable, there are others where association of
one sort or another appears to answer best. Many enterprises are on such a large scale that no single individual is
capable of understanding all the detail, and though there are
some giant industries in the hands of private individuals
there appears to be an increasing tendency to organise great
concerns by the association of several capitalists. The
tendency to turn private firms into public companies, whatever may occasion it, is one symptom of a preference which
is widely felt. The success of associations of consumers in
competing with retail shops, or the combination of rival
houses into 'trusts' so that all the business may be done on
the same lines, are other symptoms of the change. It appears
that there are numerous undertakings that can be most
conveniently conducted by means of associated capital; and
it need hardly be added that when any association becomes
so powerful as to extend to the whole country, such a scheme
of organisation must have been developed that there need be
little difficulty in buying out the capitalists and conducting
the business as a department of state, if this were desirable.
As a matter of policy, however, it may be questioned
whether the public are not likely to be better served if the
company retains its separate existence, but is carefully
controlled by public opinion in the press and Parliament.

In existing society, then, there appear to be these four

different systems in which capital is administered—*State management*, *Municipal management*, *Private management*, and *Associated management*; and these four systems of management appear to correspond to different kinds of industry, or different classes of objects, for the attainment of which capital is required. In our present régime all these various methods may exist side by side, and each undertaking may be organised on that method which seems most suitable, or which proves itself most suitable after repeated experiment.

II. Is any one Method superseding the rest?

It is not easy to say, so far as experience goes, which of these methods of management is the fittest and is most likely to outlive the rest, or whether any one has so little vitality that it is likely to be improved off the face of the earth within a comparatively brief period.

1. At first sight it seems as if 'nationalism' were winning in the race; there are certain kinds of conditions which the nation only can secure, and there is a steady movement in the formation of giant companies and trusts, while considerable pressure is being exercised in the direction of having these powerful monopolies overhauled or taken over by the State. It appears as if private capital were giving way to associated capital, and associated capital were giving way to national or public capital, and that if this movement continued or were accelerated the whole would pass under the direct management of the State.

a. But there is another change which is also in progress, and which must also be taken into account; business is assuming more and more of an international character every day, and there is more international organisation for commercial purposes. The postal union is a case in point, and bimetallists hope to furnish an instance of monetary arrangements which shall extend far beyond the limits of any one sovereign who mints coins for the use of his subjects. These are forecasts of attempts to treat the world as a whole for commercial purposes, and indeed this is habitually done.

When we examine our food supply it is extraordinary to find
how much we are dependent on foreign sources not only for
bread-stuffs, or comforts like tea and coffee, but for fresh
fruit, butter, and eggs.   Rapid communications by telegraph
or by rail and steamer have revolutionised commerce, and
enabled us to treat the world as a whole for business
purposes.   Hence the monopolists who are dreaded now
are not the engrossers who forestalled goods coming to a
town and who were put down by municipal authority in
mediaeval times, not the chartered companies or patentees
who held a monopoly throughout England and who gave rise
to outcries all through the seventeenth century, but the
rings and trusts that control the total mass of copper or
cotton or oil in the world.   In such cases there are business
operations that extend far beyond the limits and control of
any nation, and the question arises, how far is the nation
being superseded as the unit for economic purposes?   In old
days the problems were set as practical ones—how may the
power of this nation be maintained?   The subordination of
the pursuit of wealth to national power was taken for granted
by the mercantilists; the power of the nation was the end,
they studied the means.   With Adam Smith too the nation
was taken as ultimate, and those who have followed him
have written of nations as recognised economic groups,
within which there is a free flow of labour and capital.   But
may we not now regard the world as one economic realm in
which there is an easy flow of labour and capital,—freer
perhaps than there was within the limits of England in the
time of Adam Smith?   Can we assume that the nation is a
permanent economic organism, or is it destined to take a
subordinate place in the economic life of the future, as the
manor and the municipality do in the economic life of the
present?

b. There are other facts which seem to point in this direction; economic policy is no longer guided with reference to
national objects; philanthropy has a word to say, and may in
time come to have greater influence still.   There are protests
against the destruction of native races, and the exploiting of

subject populations, and a cold-blooded policy of mere national aggrandisement could hardly be pursued by any European nation now as it was followed in old days by the Romans.

Further, it appears that the differences between nations are being diminished and more connecting links are being forged. This is chiefly due to the influence of capital; English capitalists have a large stake in the prosperity of nearly every country in the world, and this is to some small extent a pledge for friendly relations. The tie is being formed, not by commercial intercourse breaking down tariffs, as Cobden hoped, but by capitalists who take advantage of foreign tariffs to transfer their enterprise. Besides this, the introduction of machinery is doing something to put different lands more nearly on a level; there is less specialisation of industry, and therefore more possibility for the fluidity of labour throughout the world. While on the one hand there are signs of the formation of international organisations for business purposes, there are on the other hand symptoms that the barriers of nationalism—for economic purposes—are breaking down.

Who shall strike a balance between these probabilities, or prove the superiority of economic organisation of any single type? On the one hand we have signs of the State undertaking more and more economic functions; on the other hand it appears that the existence of the nation, as a distinct economic group, is threatened, and that it has far less importance in the business life of to-day than it had a century ago. It is ceasing to be the centre of economic organisation, in the way that political economists usually assume, though the diminished importance now attached to problems of international trade shows that the change is recognised even by theorists. However long nations may continue as the strongholds of common laws, and common language, and common religion, of all the sentiment that binds men together and gives a common culture,—and these differences show little sign of disappearing,—the nation is no longer so clearly distinguished as formerly as a well-marked economic group.

2. At any rate it might seem that the individual control of capital is passing away; but is it so? Apart from the question of management and attention to details, it appears that there is still a field for personal energy in breaking new ground. It has been remarked by Mr. Bagehot that one reason of the success of British commerce lay in the fact that there had never been a great mercantile caste, or great mercantile families of the Italian type, but there were also interlopers who pushed their way from the ranks and broke through the stereotyped habits and old traditions. It will be shown hereafter that individual care is also instrumental in the formation of capital; and though with social changes the scope of individual management may become narrower than at present, it may yet continue to discharge certain functions better than can be done by any other method, and to have a real, even if a subordinate place, in economic life. The fact that many businesses are being transferred from individual to associated administration does not prove that the method of individual management may not survive as the fittest for certain purposes.

There are many people who are strongly impressed with the value of individual energy, and who are constantly deprecating any tendency on the part of the State to encroach on the free play of individual vigour. They deprecate State interference with individuals, and are constanly inclined to lay down limits which the State ought not to pass. There is one thing that may be said; the State ought not to try to do what individuals can do best for themselves; but only experience can determine, from time to time, how well this or that can be done by the State, and how well by individuals. The problem as to the respective spheres of the State and the individual is not capable of general solution; the State and the individual are not definite things which always stand, or ought always to stand in the same relations to one another. The individual as he comes into being is formed by the State, and is a man with certain rights and conceptions because he has been born in a State where these were current. The forms of States, too, change—tribal, municipal, national, federal, and so forth; there can hardly be any general economic propositions which will apply to all such types of State and all the members who go to form them, and under whose influence they are in turn developed and changed.

This, too, one may say; the objects in which the Government exerts itself are objects in which all the people have a part; it is with national projects that Government is concerned, and with projects which, just because they are national, concern all the citizens. Since they concern all they may seem less pressing to each man than his private affairs. It is because no man can assess the precise advantage he derives from being an Englishman instead of a native of the French province of Albion, or assess it in terms of money, that the British voter is inclined to subordinate the national projects, which concern everybody, to the petty interests of his shop, which concern no one but himself. And certainly if such a conflict of interests does arise there can be no doubt which should be forced to give way. The national projects concern the whole nation, present and future; it is far more important that such objects as England has in view should be seen to, rather than this man's shop or that man's shop should answer. State interference may be unwise—it is human to err—but there are objects for which the State may have to interfere with individual interests, or even individual life, that are of paramount importance, and that far outweigh any merely private concern.

3. There are many grounds for supposing that the municipality may take a more important place in the future than it has recently done in the past. In the thirteenth or fourteenth century each European municipality was a separate isolated institution, with its own customs and privileges, its own relations with other municipalities, and but little share or interest in the life of the nation in which it was placed. This narrow isolation has been broken down by more frequent intercourse, and the exceptional status of certain places has been superseded by the common facilities which exist throughout whole realms. In our own time there is a revival

of municipal *esprit de corps*; the political power of the provincial towns is very great; the pride of citizens in the place of their birth, or the place where they made their wealth, shows itself in gifts of parks, and galleries and churches and museums. And there is at the same time a movement in favour of a decentralisation which may give the power of administering capital for objects which have been hitherto pursued by the State into local hands. How far this decentralisation may proceed with advantage is a difficult and disputed question, but it is admitted on all sides that the power of peace and war must rest with the Central Government; and hence it follows that the administration of capital, so far as this military power is concerned, must also rest with the State. The economic functions of the municipality—in which, for convenience, I include other forms of local government—may be greatly increased, but the State cannot be altogether superseded, so far as the necessity for making provision for this contingency remains.

There are perhaps some who would contend that if separate municipalities were formed, and nations superseded, the causes of taking up arms would be diminished, and that war may therefore be left out of account. But Plato, who framed an ideal state in Greece, where there was no nation but a group of municipalities, did not find in his experience any grounds for supposing that war could be dispensed with in his ideal republic. In fact, in such conditions as he knew, or as existed later in Italy, there are more frequent reasons for war; more petty jealousies, more trivial rivalries. It is easy to conceive that if the control of common national interests and rule were removed, Liverpool might go to war with Manchester about the ship canal, and destroy the budding prosperity of Cardiff or the hopes of Milford Haven. Intermunicipal war was waged when there were causes of municipal jealousy, and national wars may continue to exist so long as there are decided national differences which give rise to international irritation.

Now, though the nation as an economic organism is less important than formerly, there are few, if any, signs that it is decaying as a political force. So long as there are differences of natural products there will be trade between different countries ; and though such interconnexion gives ties between distant nations it also may serve to occasion jealousies and wars. Very many of the most terrible wars the world has seen have been partly, at least, commercial wars ; and so long as international commerce remains, there are likely to be occasions for misunderstanding and irritation and quarrels.

National differences, too, which are due partly to differences of race and language and religion and history, show but little signs of dying out. Some striking evidence on this matter is alleged to be found in the United States. There is no real proof of closer amalgamation between the black and white races in the south. The half castes die out, and the pure blacks and pure whites are perpetuated with but few signs of fusion. In different parts of the States and of Canada, French districts, or German districts, or Irish districts, or Scottish districts may be found, and thus the national differences of the Old World have reappeared in the New. So far as the constitution and government of the United States are concerned there has been every effort to absorb these separate settlements into a government which claims to rest on the freedom and equality of men. Even if these different emigrant settlements do amalgamate completely in the course of time, we may yet feel that natural differences which have been able to reappear in the New World are likely to die hard in the Old. The municipality may extend its economic powers at the expense of the nation, but there is no likelihood that it will supersede it altogether.

III. Industrial Organisation.

We thus are forced to recognise that each of these methods of administering capital appears to be able to justify its existence, and will probably maintain itself, as the best method of fulfilling some function in our economic life. Cosmopolitan and international organisations may grow from the mere germs we now see, and municipal institutions may expand, but it seems improbable that national economic life will wholly disappear; so too there may be some scope for the individual capitalist, however much joint-stock companies multiply.

The present social system gives opportunity for administering capital according to any of these plans, whichever answers best; it also gives freedom for trying a new method, if that seems likely to prove preferable. The respective spheres of national and municipal and individual and associated administration are always changing, as new wants or new discoveries affect the organisation of different industries. Whatever is likely to be the best means of controlling capital, so as to meet requirements then and there, can be easily brought into play.

1. Those who are impatient with the social arrangements of our own time are easily able to point out economic defects in this or that direction, through the misuse or waste of capital. There is a terrible waste which arises in the course of reckless competition—in cutting prices and in bankruptcy, even in advertising; there is waste, since there does not seem to be any adequate return to the community. In the same way it is often urged that there is no adequate return to the community for all the wealth sunk in land, and that landlords' rents and royalties would afford a far more general return if they were held by the State or by municipalities. There are many who desire to substitute organisation for competition, and thus to do away with the recognised evils of the present system. Of course, if it is really to supersede competition altogether, the organisation must be very thoroughgoing and complete, so as to leave no scope for any individualistic passions and ambitions, and to call forth feelings of quite a different type. This is, briefly put, the aim of socialists, and there is much in their criticism of existing institutions which shows that there are many faults which call for remedy.

2. We are, however, justified in asking any professed socialist what *type* of administration he suggests as the basis for the thoroughgoing organisation which he desires? In-

dividualistic and associated administration rest on competition; these are apparently excluded; but does he favour
cosmopolitan or national or municipal organisation?

Now, just as it is easy to find flaws in existing social
arrangements, so it is easy to pick holes in any projected
one; and socialistic schemes have had no immunity from
criticism. To such criticism of details the socialist is apt
to reply that after all these are mere minor matters which
could be arranged if the broad outlines of the scheme were
adopted. This is very true, but it is also true that there
must be some details; and the fundamental defect in
socialistic proposals is this,—that whatever scheme was
adopted it must in some of its details be inferior to the
present system. The thoroughgoing system must adopt one
type of administration; whichever type is preferred, and
carried out with rigid consistency, there would be a real loss
from discarding the other types, each of which shows itself
fitted for the administration of certain departments. If the
national type were adopted there would be loss through
over-centralisation; if a municipal type, there would be the
loss of the control that is exercised by common opinions and
interests, and the jarring of pretty rivalries and antagonisms.
In either case there would be a loss of the enterprise which
displays itself in the individual and associated management
of capital.

3. The socialist may contend, indeed, that it is not the share
of material gain he looks to, but the moral advance. But, after
all, material progress gives the *opportunity* of moral advance;
if material progress is checked there will not be the same opportunity for moral advance. Is it possible for him to contend
that under socialism the lesser opportunities will be turned to
better account? That it gives a nobler ideal, a better discipline for the individual, and therefore a deeper spiritual power?
Those who believe that perfect gifts come from above and are
received by men will not hope that any new method of organising society, any more widely diffused comfort, will in itself
call forth such noble aspirations, or discipline such unselfish
characters, as shall help man to rise to a really higher level.

PART II

PRACTICAL QUESTIONS.

—•■•—

CHAPTER VI.

The Formation of Capital.

Capital has been already defined as a fund from which the owner expects to get an income. It is not necessary to try and justify this definition: it may suffice for us to use it and see how far it justifies itself. Capital is a word in popular use; if we wish to give more clearness and accuracy to discussions of popular subjects it is convenient to use the word as nearly as possible in the sense which it commonly conveys, but to use it with more precision. A great many economists have not been sufficiently careful in either respect. They have fixed attention on capital devoted to industry, and have spoken as if a man's wealth ceased to be capital if it was not devoted to the production of more wealth. Thus a man who holds brewery shares has capital, but if he ceases to hold these shares and buys consols, although he continues to obtain an income, he would, according to many definitions, cease to be a capitalist. Popular language does not recognise this distinction; the man has capital and changes his investment, but does not convert capital into non-capital thereby; and the text-books would have done better if they had tried to adhere to popular usage in this matter. But there has also been some confusion, because after fixing on an accidental quality to mark out capital, they have not always adhered to that definition with precision; there is an overwhelming temptation to extend the use of terms by analogy till they are emptied of all definite meaning. We shall do best if we define capital not by what it generally does, nor what it usually consists of, nor by the manner in which it is obtained, but by what it brings to the owner. The owner may make a mistake and use it in a way in which it yields no income, but he always intends to get an income, and expects it when he invests; and the bringing in of an income is, subject to this limitation, a feature which marks all capital, however it is got, and however it is used. Taking then this definition, we wish to see if we can keep strictly to it, and in so doing discuss the various questions connected with the formation and use of capital with precision. In so far as this can be done, the definition will have justified itself, for its two parts contain references to each of these topics,—the formation of a fund and the application of the fund so as to get an income.

I. Conditions for the Formation of Capital.

You cannot form a fund of wealth unless certain social conditions are present, and unless there are certain personal powers and certain opportunities. The same conditions which are requisite for the formation of any fund of wealth at all, will also favour the formation of larger and larger amounts of capital, if they are present in increased force and effectiveness.

1. There can be no question of saving up a fund of wealth, unless there is some sort of security for enjoying it. Continual warfare and pillage must produce a state of society in which the possession of wealth is a mere temptation to attack, and in many ages men have preferred to appear poor even when they really were comfortably off, in order to escape the jealous interference of powerful neighbours. The nature of the social sanctions which give protection to hoards of property is not always very intelligible. Certain Kafir tribes can leave under-

ground stores of food in tracts where other tribes wander freely, without any apprehension that they will be pillaged, though it is not easy to see what gives these pits immunity. In the early middle ages, when private wars were so rife, kings were glad to commit their treasure to the care of a knightly order, and the Temple at Paris served as a bank of deposit both for Philip Augustus and for John Lackland. Every improvement in government which renders a man's property, be it large or small, more secure to him, gives an increased facility for forming funds of wealth. Whether this is brought about by greater security from hostile invasion, by greater immunity from the attacks of thieves and robbers, by greater care in the levying of taxes, or by improved judicial administration, the result will be the same, and there will be fewer obstacles to the formation of hoards of wealth.

2. But after all these are somewhat negative conditions; there are certain personal qualities which are the active force in the formation of capital. Social environment counts for much, but it is not everything. Just as we have seen that the environment of physical circumstances affects the development of society, while the personal qualities of skill and enterprise enable men to take a further step forward beyond the limits imposed by circumstances, so it appears that the social environment is not unimportant (as it limits the exercise of the power of saving, or on the other hand gives it scope), but that the mainspring from which additional hoards arise is found in personal dispositions and qualities. The man who can look forward, who can put off till to-morrow what he might enjoy to-day, is the man who forms a fund of wealth, and this is the disposition which is the most active and operative element in all formation of capital.

There are many men in whom this disposition is weak; there are others in whom by character and association it seems to be wanting, and it differs curiously in different races. In India there is a striking contrast between the Parsee and the Hindu in this respect. The Parsee accumulates wealth to use in trade; the Hindu will gladly spend his available wealth and run into debt at some family or caste festival; he wishes to be remembered as a man who behaved handsomely, but he has no desire to rise in the world. He wants to be well thought of in the circle in which he lives, and does not wish to rise out of it. It is not necessary to compare these two dispositions from a moral point of view; one may be more sociable and pleasanter than the other; and the Parsee is never likely to be a popular man. It is enough to point out that the Hindu is less likely to amass capital than the Parsee, not because he has less opportunity and the social conditions differ, but because his personal ambitions and aspirations are of a distinctly different type. There are many servant girls whose love of dress is so strong that they can't save; and there are many folk who are unable to amass anything because of their love of eating and drinking. Personal vanity or greed and sociability may be the grounds of present expenditure which interferes with the formation of hoards; and the man who can't save may have many excellent qualities which are denied to the man who can. He may be a good Christian and a kind husband and father, a just master, a generous friend, and an accomplished man, but he does not become rich or get on. If we leave him on one side with this tribute of respect, it is not because we disparage him or think more highly of the men who get on, but merely because the men who get on and become rich are the topic before us, and the other people are not. The generous friend who is badly off is a better human being than the man who has money but who is not generous and has no friends, but he is not the subject in hand. He is left on one side not because he is despicable or unimportant, but merely because he is irrelevant. His economic influence has been already alluded to as most beneficial in helping to keep up our ideals, and thus to raise the whole social tone of society. We want now to note the disposition that is effective in forming hoards, and the man who does not form hoards does not concern us for the present. The whole series of moral questions may be left over till later; we do not wish to see whether hoards are right, or to what extent they are right, or how they are to be formed in the right place and the right time and with the right end in view ; we are merely considering the practical question how they are formed at all, and the active force which has most effect in this respect is the power of postponing present enjoyment for the sake of a larger accumulation in the future,—what is commonly called the desire of saving.

This power of saving involves certain intellectual and moral qualities. It requires a certain amount of imagination to foresee the advantage which will accrue from the possession of a hoard ; this is probably the difficulty with certain savages, to whom the prospect of an entirely changed life, with diminished liberty, offers no attractions, even though it should afford more regular supplies of food. It might be more comfortable, but it would certainly be less diverting. Besides this power of imagination, there must also be strength of will; the object in view is a distant one, and there is no little difficulty in pursuing it steadily for a long time. This is the quality in which children are often lacking; there is no deficiency of power to realise the things they can get by saving. A boy desires a pair of pads, and he wishes for them more keenly whenever his shins are hit by a fast ball, or when he is bowled because he shirked it; but it takes a long time to save, and the attractions of caramels and butter-scotch are strong.

a. But of these two elements, the power of imagination and the power of will, the latter is far more important in our state of society, or indeed in any state of society where there is the hoarding not merely of wealth, but of wealth in a form that is fluid and can be applied in any direction, that is, of capital. What is required in this case is the accumulation of money,—of many coins, or of a sum represented by four figures at the bankers,—and that is an object which can be grasped by a mind with very little imaginative or poetic faculty. On the whole, in our modern life it is in strength of will that the secret of accumulation lies, and the man who has risen, the self-made man, the successful millionaire, is likely to be distinguished by this quality and to value himself highly upon it. And sentimentalists are merely foolish to disparage it because they do not find that it is always accompanied by other moral or intellectual qualities which they appreciate better.

b. In so far however as the desire to save depends on power of forecasting the future it is worth while to notice that there are two distinct sorts of advantage in the future which appeal to men of somewhat different types, or who are somewhat differently placed. Some save because they wish to have a reserve fund, and some save because they wish to have an income, or to have a larger income; so at least it would seem. That the latter is a real and distinct motive may be doubted; on the other hand, it is often spoken of as if it were the sole motive for saving. It is surely obvious however that the chief motive in saving a hoard is the desire to have a hoard to fall back on, and not the desire to have an income. The desire to have an income is a potent force in determining the investment of capital; but the man who saves, desires to have a fund of wealth apart altogether from the way in which he uses it. Thus in primitive times a tribe will hoard a reserve of food, as the Germans did in the days of Tacitus. So with the artisan who makes small savings in the present day; he is anxious to accumulate £50, not because he will be so much the better of twenty-five shillings annual income, but because he will have a good round sum to fall back upon in bad times. The investor must submit at times to reductions of income, but he can hope that things will take a turn; what he really dreads is loss of the principal or capital. Hence the chief motive in saving is not so much the desire to have interest, as the desire to have principal. It will yield an income, but it also affords a substantial reserve on which it is possible for a man to fall back in any case of necessity.

There are some cases in which the motive for saving appears to be that of enjoying a larger income later on. This appears to be the case when a man endows his life and pays £150 a year for five and twenty years in order to enjoy the interest on £4000 in the last twenty years of his life, when his power of earning is decreasing; but such postponed

enjoyment of income does not appear to be such an effective
motive as the desire to have a reserve to fall back upon.
This is the commonest motive for saving, even in pre-
capitalist times, and it is a very real motive for saving in the
present day. It is the motive to which all trades unions and
friendly societies appeal. They do not give their members
an annual income, although they exact annual payments;
but they do give immunity from anxiety about a greater or
smaller number of the risks of life. Some will secure a man
against the losses consequent on ill-health or give him benefits in old age; others provide for him in cases where he is
temporarily out of employment. But the advantage which
accrues to the member is not that of a regular income, but
of a reserve on which he can draw in any of the ordinary
emergencies of life.

This is the real class distinction in the present day; the
most important distinction between the classes and the masses.
In old days no one was secure against physical risks; his
wealth, however great, might disappear suddenly like that
of Job, or the Merchant of Venice. But the facilities for
dividing investment, so as not to put all the eggs in one
basket, together with the opportunities of insurance and
obtaining security against various specific risks, are so
numerous, that it is possible for the rich man to make
provision for wife and children so as to secure them against
all ordinary risks of falling into poverty at any period in the
whole course of their lives. But a considerable portion of
the artisan classes, and the whole of the unorganised
labourers, enjoy no such freedom from anxiety; they rarely
can see their way clearly for more than a week or two, and
there are constant risks to health from exposure or accident,
which may throw them into the extremest poverty at any
moment. Only those who understand how great this risk is,
and how much their comparatively small reserves separate
the organised from the unorganised employees, can realise the
immense importance for comfort in life of possessing a
reserve fund, and how immensely important this desire is in
connexion with the formation of capital.

The assumption sometimes made that men save, not for the sake of possessing a reserve fund but for the sake of enjoying income, has been the basis of some argument that seems to me illusory. It is said that the rate of interest is declining, and that if it gets very low the motive for saving will be gone, and that we can look for no more additions to capital. Even this does not appear to be conclusive; if the rate of interest falls, the man who desires to have a large income will have to save more so as to enjoy the annual return he desires. If interest falls on the best security from 3 to 2 per cent. he will have to save £15,000 instead of £10,000 in order to enjoy £300 a year, so that a fall of interest might lead to increased efforts to save. But if the chief motive to save, the one which has appealed to human beings over the longest period, and appeals most widely to all classes of the community, is not the desire to save but the desire to have a reserve fund, then a fall in the rate of interest will not affect the desire to save at all; this will remain as strong as before, and accumulation might continue unchecked even if the rate of interest were merely nominal. It would only be appreciably affected if men were forced to make payments in order to have their hoards securely kept for them.

c. All human beings may be credited with a certain amount of imagination, and a certain power of will; but in many these traits are but imperfectly developed. The object of the facilities for saving, which are provided by governments or by philanthropists, is to render the practice easier to those in whom the disposition to save is not strong. The ordinary goose club is the least pretentious and most generally attractive of all such schemes, for the object appeals to the uncultivated imagination; the necessary saving is not unduly prolonged, so that there is no great strain upon the resolution; and the amount of 'present enjoyment' which the man foregoes is overlooked in the attractions of the public house. In fact it offers such complete facilities that it hardly calls forth the faculty or helps men to form the habit of saving.

Many schemes for facilitating the habit of saving depend

for their success on the way in which they enable people to
take advantage of trivial occasions, and thus help them not
to miss the opportunities of saving that come within their
reach. It is of course impossible to say how far by providing
opportunities the latent disposition to save is called forth
and stimulated; and those in whom the disposition is strong
will save on the smallest opportunity. At the same time,
though we cannot say how much is due to social, how much
to personal, and how much to physical surroundings, it is not
clear that the whole of the conditions which affect the result
can be stated in terms of any one of the three; but for the
sake of completeness it is worth while to look at the matter
from the physical, as well as from the personal and social
side.

3. The opportunity to save occurs when a man is in
possession of a superfluity of wealth of a kind which he can
accumulate. He can take advantage of a time of plenty, and
he can take the fullest advantage of it if he can lay up a kind
of possession which will keep without spoiling.

a. In regard to the primitive saving of laying up a reserve
fund of food, it is obvious that it will take place at one time
of the year, after harvest; and that, if the population has
increased up to the limits given by the available food in
ordinary years, it will only occur occasionally when food is
particularly plentiful. Without the seven years of plenty
Joseph could hardly have accumulated a store to serve during
seven years of famine.

Similarly in modern times the best opportunity for saving
occurs at times of prosperity; if a man counts to get ten per
cent. on the capital in any business, and he finds that he
has made fifteen per cent., he is able to put away the sum
which represents five per cent. on his capital. If he only
gets his ten per cent. he will keep the business going, but he
makes no additional accumulations. This is the fact which
has been noticed by the Manchester school of economists,
who have laid stress on high profits as a sign of prosperity,
and treated high profits (and high interest) as a motive to
the increase of capital. Such a state of affairs does not give

a strong motive, but it gives an opportunity: everybody knows that the high prices and large returns will not last for ever, and that the additions to capital will not permanently or even long secure an addition to income at this large rate. But everybody in business sees that he can lay aside a large sum (to be used in his own business or another), and he makes the most of the opportunity while it lasts. In this way high profits indicate a very real element of prosperity; they show a state of affairs when capital is being accumulated by many men, and therefore they show that increased facilities for industry and commerce are available on many sides. When, on the other hand, the rate of profit is low in most industries, there may be many men who are anxious to save, but who have no opportunity, or no opportunity of saving on a large scale. From this point of view we may see that there is an element of truth in the position taken by Rodbertus and others, who have decried the assertion that capital is the result of saving; no, they say, it is the result of diligence. It is diligence which gives a man a superfluity of goods, and therefore without diligence he would have nothing to lay aside and hoard. Undoubtedly diligence is often, though not always, the means of bringing a superfluity into existence, and thus it provides the opportunity for saving. But there must be the desire of a fund in the future and the will to wait for it, or the opportunity which diligence provides will be allowed to slip. The virtues of thrift and diligence often go together, but for all that the part which each plays in the formation of hoards is perfectly distinguishable.

b. The possibility of amassing wealth also depends on the kinds of commodity which are available. Keep a thing seven years, it is said, and you will find a use for it, but there are some things which will not last very long and cannot be kept. It is impossible to hoard milk for long, even when converted into cheese, and woollen goods are apt to be injured; the Tartar on the Steppes has no possessions which will keep, and he cannot be expected to form stores. On the other hand, if corn is kept dry and protected from rats, it may be preserved without destruction for centuries, as in the case of the Egyptian wheat; but the precious metals and jewels are among the least destructible forms of wealth, and they therefore lend themselves most readily to hoarding. The precious metals from their divisibility too can be laid aside as the opportunity occurs, and the man or woman of thrifty habits will be able to accumulate the most trifling sums till the stocking or the tea-pot contains a considerable amount.   So far as divisibility is concerned this holds good of any kind of circulating medium, or of the forms of credit. The most extraordinary example of this is found in the history of the great co-operative societies; they enjoy a plethora of capital, but these large accumulations are chiefly formed by laying aside the discounts for cash payments on small purchases.   The success of these societies is chiefly due to the fact that they have given the artisan a new opportunity for saving, by enabling him to accumulate the money that is due to him for paying cash; these fractional sums are scarcely missed at the time, and can therefore be easily spared, but they accumulate to a large amount in the course of years.

There are certain commodities which appear at first sight to be specially adapted for saving because they can not only be kept, but they actually improve by keeping.   It is on this account that some men invest in pictures by young and unknown artists, in the belief that they will increase in value as the men become famous.   So, too, first editions, early impressions, may all come to have a fancy value, and they are on this account legitimate objects of speculation. Another instance, which specially attracted the attention of MacCulloch, was that of wine, which will, of course, improve if it is judiciously selected and laid down.   But these cases rather fall under the investment of wealth than the formation of hoards; they are instances not of saving, but of speculation.   A poor man may gradually accumulate a very valuable collection, by patience and skill, but collectors rarely forecast public taste in such fashion as to make their favourite hobby pay.   The purchase of such objects are generally speculations in which men engage who have some wealth, not means of accumulation, and commodities of this kind are not by their very nature generally available as offering opportunities for saving. They differ, too, from other employments of capital, because the owner expects to get, not so much an income, as a sum which may be equivalent to many years income; there is no difference of principle between this and any other commercial speculation; but the man who tries to get a gain by continuing to hold an improving capital must be willing to lie out of his capital for a long time. Thus the man who lays down £100 worth of port sinks his money; he does not receive any income from it, and the gain only accrues when he realises his investment and sells at a profit; his capital is sunk, and just because it is sunk and the opportunity of realising it may not easily occur, this form of investment is one that many capitalists would eschew. These exceptional cases do not afford opportunities for forming hoards, and the gain which comes from them differs in a marked degree from the income which is derived from capital.

c. In whatever way the saving is effected, however, a fund of commodities is formed or rights to use commodities are acquired. This has, indeed, given rise to the opinion that capital has no independent existence as an economic factor. Its very existence is said to be owing to previous labour, and the profits, it is urged, should go to the labour that made it possible. All capital does indeed consist of commodities, and labour is an element in the production of commodities; but by insisting on a quality which is common to all commodities, we do not get help in distinguishing those commodities which are used as capital from those commodities which are not. Without previous labour capital could not be formed, for there would be no opportunity for forming it; this may be admitted at once, but it is not formed by labour alone, but by saving exercised upon the results of past labour. Those who were anxious to find some external note by which they might exclude land from the scope of capital have been apt to say that capital consisted of the products of past labour, and this has given

rise to the opinion that there is a mere juggle by which a
portion of the products of labour are somehow, without
undergoing further physical change, transmuted into a sub-
stance called capital. But this transmutation, though it does
not affect the physical form of the commodities hoarded, is
not a mere juggle. Like all other economic and social
processes, it is primarily due to what human beings think
and determine; it is in the mind of the possessor that the
distinction between capital and non-capital really lies, and it
is from the purpose of the possessor, and not from the genesis
of the material he hoards, that the formation of capital really
proceeds. The possession of material goods renders it
possible to hoard; some kinds of goods lend themselves to
hoarding more easily than others, but they do not hoard
themselves; there must be human foresight and human
determination, or goods will not accumulate.

II. The Things which Capital Denotes.

So far we have insisted on the fact that capital is a fund
of wealth, and have noted the conditions, the dispositions,
and the opportunities which co-operate for the formation of
capital. It remains for us to consider how far this view
of the formation of capital gives us any light in regard to
property or powers which are in some respects analogous
to capital, and about which there is much dispute as to
whether they are capital or not.

1. *Personal Capital.*—It is sometimes said that a man's
acquired skill is his capital. It may have analogies to capital
in that it enables him to get a larger income, but the analogy
is with capital sunk in land, not with capital as a separate
possession. Just as a man who improves his estate gets
an increased rental, so the man who improves himself gets
increased wages, but the gain comes as wages, and not as
income apart from wages. It is increased or diminished by
the causes that affect the rate of wages rather than by those
that affect the rate of profits.

But in any case skill is not a fund. It is not of the nature of a hoard on which a man can fall back in case of an emergency; it is not wealth that can be realised apart from the man himself. The man with capital who falls into bad health and cannot work need not starve, but the man who has skill but cannot work will not be able to subsist on his skill. And it certainly is not got by accumulation; by exercising his faculties, such as they are, a man learns to use them better; but it is by using them and not by hoarding them that the results accrue. There may be self-discipline in acquiring skill as there is in acquiring capital, but the opportunities that occur for forming capital will not necessarily be opportunities for acquiring skill; it does not arise through putting by a surplus.

In fact, though we habitually speak of a man as possessing skill, it may be doubted whether skill is really a 'possession' at all; it is the man who is skilful, his skill is part of himself; the term includes qualities of his mind or body; a man can exchange his possessions for money, and when he does he parts with them; but when a man gains by the exercise of his skill he does not part with it; he has it still. The man hires himself, and he receives larger or smaller hire according as he is a skilful man or no; but his skill is not a possession which will bring gain apart from himself, or which he accumulates by refraining from using his powers, or which supplies a reserve fund in case of sickness or accident. The analogy to capital is of the slightest; it is most near, perhaps, in those stories of mediaeval gentlemen who sold themselves to the devil on condition of obtaining an income and living like princes; they used themselves to purchase for themselves a terminable annuity.

There have of course been many states of society where human skill was a possession, but just because the human beings were not their own masters, but were the slaves of their proprietors. A man may keep a training stable as a source of income; he may devote his capital to the breeding and training of horses, and of course he is engaged in a business like any other business, and the products he has to sell are highly trained horses. In exactly the same way a man may devote himself to the breeding and training of slaves. It has rarely been a remunerative business, as the breeders have had to compete in markets largely supplied with the captives of war or piracy; but it was a recognised department of rural economy on Roman estates, and Columella describes the management of the baby farm as he did that of the dairy farm or anything else. At any place or time when human beings were recognised objects of exchange owned by proprietors, they might be considered as a form in which capital was invested, and a gang of slaves is a fund of wealth. A gang of highly skilled and reliable slaves was a much more valuable possession than a gang of stupid and dishonest slaves, and represented a far larger capital. But the skill of a free man is not an object he possesses; it is one of his own qualities, and it cannot be properly described as part of his capital.

2. There is still more difficulty about the phrase *national capital*. The national capital would by analogy consist of all the national possessions from which the nation expects to get an income; all industry and commerce afford the sources whence income is derived, and if all the elements that are necessary to carry on national industry are regarded as national possessions, the land and the population would alike be considered parts of the national capital. It may appear perhaps that the citizens cannot be named the possessions of the nation, but in so far as they can be called upon to arm in defence of the nation, and to risk their lives, they certainly appear to be very completely and perhaps unwillingly controlled by the nation, and to be used by the nation for its objects. They can even be the subjects of exchange, when a piece of territory with its inhabitants is ceded to another power, as in the recent cases of Elsass and Lothringen, of Savoy and Nice, or Heligoland. Just as a man's capital consists of the possessions alive or dead, slaves or beasts or steam engines, from which he expects an income; so by analogy the national capital might be said to consist of all the possessions, alive or dead, from which the State directly or indirectly obtains a revenue.

a. At the same time, when we follow out the analogy in this way, it appears that national capital differs so much from private capital that it is inconvenient to use the same term for both. National Capital, strictly taken, would include the land and its conditions of climate and soil, the population and its various qualities, as well as the funds of wealth which constitute the capital of individuals. It seems better to discard a name which may give rise to such confusion, and to speak of the sources of revenue as the national resources rather than as the national capital. The kinds of things that can be owned and possessed, and therefore that can be parts of a fund of wealth, are pretty clearly marked if we confine our attention to individual wealth in countries where slavery does not exist. The resources of the nation include many things which cannot be thus appropriated by individuals; and it is, to say the least, unnecessary to insist on expanding the term capital by analogy to include national possessions, which have a sufficiently good name of their own already.

b. Instead of following out the analogy in the thorough manner adopted above, some writers think it convenient to use the term national capital for funds of kinds of wealth such as individuals might possess—material, exchangeable goods. The question then arises whether the national capital had best be taken to include the aggregate of individual capitals, or whether it shall be limited to the fund of material marketable objects from which the nation derives an income.

If we take it in the larger sense there is considerable difficulty in adding up the total of individual capital so as not to count the same funds twice over; this is of course due to the manner in which capital is lent. There is a danger of reckoning the fund of wealth which Brown uses, and then reckoning over again the fund of wealth which Smith has lent him to use. Consols represent a large amount of wealth lent to the Government; this is part of the aggregate of individual wealth, but it is a national debt and not a national asset. The question is still further confused by the individual wealth lent to foreign nations. Till such difficulties as these are satisfactorily settled on some clear

principle, there can be little advantage in trying to sum up
the amount of the national capital.   In any case ' the aggregate of individual capital' is a term which would serve the
purpose clearly.

The remaining sense of the term National Capital occurs
when it is applied to the fund of material marketable commodities owned not by individuals but by the nation, and
from which the nation derives an income.   There is of course
much national property which does not fall under this category; the Houses of Parliament and the Tower of London
may be regarded as national possessions, but they are not
used as sources of income, except to a limited extent.   The
various naval and military arsenals may be included by a
stretch of the term, as they save expenditure that would
otherwise be incurred.   Public works like the great irriga-
tion canals in India are a source of revenue, but the capital
employed in constructing them is sunk; they can hardly be
regarded as a form of capital, but as a form of property in
which capital has been sunk.   As a matter of fact there is
very little such national capital in any nation.   There is but
little in the way of national reserve funds; and very little
national wealth is used for the purpose of securing more
national income.   There are national resources which have
been improved with capital, but outside the organisation of
the Post Office there is very little remunerative ' national
capital' in England.

III. The Dependence of the State on Borrowed Capital.

It is worth while to insist on this point, for it appears that
when a nation wishes to have capital with which to improve
its resources it is forced to rely on the capital of private
individuals.   It may borrow the money, as is commonly done
now, or it may grant certain concessions to a capitalist or
capitalists as the Romans did.   But such capital, though
applied to national purposes, has not ceased to be individual
capital.   It is, after all, a fund which has been saved by
individuals: the property is vested in individuals, and in-

dividuals derive an income from it, though the nation expects an advantage which may or may not be measurable in terms of money.

1. The fact that the nation depends so much on obtaining the use of their capital from individuals raises an interesting question as to how far a nation as such is likely to be able to accumulate hoards and form capital at all. There have of course been large accumulations of treasure acquired by governments at particular times, but that was for the most part due to special efforts on the part of an individual monarch like Henry VII, or special opportunities like that which enabled Bismarck to secure a vast amount of gold at the expense of France. There have been monarchs who have been able to impress their thrifty disposition on the policy of the realm, and there have been statesmen who have seized the occasion of some military triumph to amass a reserve; but such monarchs and statesmen have been few. The spoils of war not infrequently slip through the hands of the successful soldiery in unproductive consumption, and the motives which most generally call forth saving do not greatly appeal to nations in their corporate capacity. The failure of sinking funds and the slow progress made in the reduction of the national debt during a period of unexampled prosperity, show, only too clearly, that there is no strong enthusiasm for relieving posterity from the burden of debt; far less are there signs of any desire to maintain heavy taxes in the present and so accumulate a reserve. It is not easy to get the populace to do anything for posterity, for posterity has never done anything for them. Hence a desire to form a reserve, which is the effective motive in the formation of private capital, does not appeal to the national imagination, and it is difficult to keep the national will at this pitch of heroic self-sacrifice. So long as there was an absolute monarch who desired to found a dynasty, the motive for accumulating treasure was similar to that of the private individual who wishes to provide for his family; but nations have not very frequent opportunities to save,—they hardly feel the motive at all.

2. This speculation as to the power of nations to form hoards which can be used as capital is an important point for socialists to take into account. The so-called nationalisation of railways, in so far as it has taken place, has been effected, not by the extinction of private capital, but by borrowing private capital to enable the nation to buy out private owners. Of course the affair can be so financed that the claims of the national creditors should be gradually paid off and the railways remain with the State; but supposing the existing means of production were thus nationalised, is it clear that the State would be able to do more than keep them going? Would it have the motive and the opportunity for forming capital as a reserve fund, i. e. to be drawn on for the expenses of government in case of the revenue falling short, or for the purpose of attempting new enterprises? The State has often had to rely on Jews or Lombards or other bankers in order to pay its way, or to meet expenses while taxes were being collected; would it be so organised as to dispense with occasional aid from capitalists, or would it be able to form large reserve funds for itself? Experience seems to show that the State will not easily develope a faculty for saving; and that just as the private capitalist may always survive as the most efficient administrator where there are many petty details to be looked to, so too he will survive as the organ by which new supplies of capital are most readily formed, even though when formed this capital should be borrowed by the State and used for public purposes.

IV. The definition reconsidered.

1. A brief retrospect may enable us to test the definition with which we started, and see how far it has given us a distinct idea of the nature of the economic power we are about to examine in some detail. It is in some ways a narrower use of the term than is current in text-books; for it hardly seems worth while to retain the division ' national capital ' at all when we discard that term as a name for national resources, and for the aggregate of private capital;

there is very little to which the term can be applied. So far as the nation uses capital it relies on private capital, and additional supplies of capital are forthcoming, not from the savings of the State as such, but from the funds of wealth accumulated by individuals. In fact the phrase appears to have been invented not as the name of any observed phenomenon, but in order to give completeness to the subject, and because the ordinary analysis of wealth seemed to require it. 'If capital,' it might be urged, 'is a requisite of the production of wealth, and there is such a thing as national wealth, then there must be such a thing as national capital to produce it.' Such appears to be the argument, but capital is not always necessary to the production of wealth, and even if it were, national wealth might be produced by the use of private capital. A similar ratiocination may have given rise to the inconvenient phrase 'personal capital,'—the labourer produces wealth, but if capital is a requisite of production, there must be capital somewhere; and so that name is sometimes given to the labourer's skill.

2. It has been my endeavour to steer clear of these dangerous analogies, and to keep to the common-sense meaning of the term. What may perhaps seem least defensible in popular phraseology is the manner in which capital sunk in land is treated as merged in land, and lost in land, and therefore not as capital at all; but at least it may be said that there is some confirmation for this view of the case. The moneyed interest of capitalists is generally distinguishable, and often opposed to that of the landed interest, because the one has a much more permanent stake in the country than the other, and is interested in developing the resources of the estate, or in enjoying it, not merely in deriving income from it. The conditions which favour agriculture may not be suitable for industry and commerce; there are real economic differences, to which is due a conflict of interest that has broken out over and over again, from the time when the distinction was first noticed in parliamentary politics to the great struggle over the corn laws. But the capitalist who retires from business and sinks his capital in land is apt

to pass over from the moneyed interest to the landed interest; his tastes and wishes and expectations take a different character. And hence while it is true that capital which is sunk in land is still wealth, it is also true to say that since it has been sunk in land it has ceased to be that kind of wealth which is ordinarily called capital, and that the income it affords to the landlord, which we call rent, is governed by very different principles from those which explain the variations in profit or the interest on loans.

(*a*) Mill has pointed out that the distinction between capital and non-capital depends on the intentions of the owner, and the application of this principle requires that a distinction should be drawn between ' Capital' and ' Land,' even though both are in a sense wealth, and both afford income. The landlord in England does not in a usual way work his estate for income only, but partly as a means of social enjoyment, and as giving prestige and so forth. He embellishes and improves it, and spends, in planting it, money which he never expects to see again, but which may provide a valuable possession for his son. The whole range of motives and interests is different from that of the millowner, who is trying to push his trade, and who buys a bit of land, the site of his mill, with the view of using it in connexion with his business. The difference lies not in the things owned, but in the intentions of the owner, and the way he deals with them. There are many men connected with the land who are capitalists; farmers who work for an annual return in a saleable product, speculators who pick up properties in the hope of selling them again at a profit, and their economic action is closely allied to that of other capitalists. There may be landlords who work the estate simply as a pecuniary speculation, and who have no interest in the land except as it yields an income in money; but so long as this is not generally the case, and the motives which actuate a landowner are very distinct from those which actuate manufacturers or merchants, there is a justification for the popular usage which classifies his property under a separate heading. It is further confirmed by the fact that the genesis of economic rent is so different from that of interest on loans or reward for enterprise, and that the value of land accrues so differently from the increase of capital that the two must be treated apart. Land might be described for economic purposes as a property in certain natural materials or powers which the owner continues to hold partly for enjoyment and partly for the sake of income. It therefore does not exactly fall under either half of the definition of capital.

(*b*) Mill's principle calls attention to a point of fundamental importance. It is true that capital consists of material things, and not of mental powers, but it is also true that material things have not the property of being capital in themselves. They have no economic property in themselves, but only in relation to human beings; a thing has no use in itself, but only if there is someone to use it; it has no exchange value in itself, but only if there is someone who wishes to obtain it in exchange; there is no intrinsic usefulness or intrinsic value in any material commodity. And in the same way there is no intrinsic quality that renders any commodity capital; whether it is capital or not depends on the man who owns it. The distinction could only be drawn with certainty in all cases if we knew exactly the views and intentions of each owner, but it is precise, so far as our knowledge of circumstances enables us to apply it. That which is not a material possession cannot be part of a hoard, and so cannot be capital; but as the forming of a hoard depends on personal qualities, and as the use of a hoard as capital depends on personal preferences, the distinction between capital and non-capital can only be clearly stated when we fix our attention on the minds of the possessor and not on the things he possesses and uses. If he uses his wealth as part of a fund from which he hopes to obtain income it is capital. If he sinks his fund in lands so as to obtain more rent it is sunk capital, and it gives an improved estate. If he uses it to get a better education it is sunk in his own improved faculties, and he can earn higher wages; but in neither case does it remain as capital.

CHAPTER VII.

The Investment of Capital.

I. Lending Money and Engaging in Enterprise.

Though capital is wealth which can be realised in money and transferred, it does not usually consist of money, but of other forms of wealth in which it has been invested. We may leave out of account for the present those kinds of wealth in which it is sunk, and from which there is no expectation of getting a regular, but only an accumulated income,—improving properties, such as building-land or wine; in these a wealthy man may speculate, but he locks up his capital and does not look for annual income. We merely want to consider the investments at which a man will look who is anxious to obtain an income without sacrificing his principal; and it is obvious on the face of it that he will expect to get some return. Stated in most general fashion it appears that there is a superior attractiveness about having a thing now, rather than having it next year. The child who is asked whether it would rather have an apple now or two apples next year would probably prefer the apple now; and the man who lends his money or invests his money now will only consent to do it because he counts on having more money or a bigger stock of goods next year. Ordinary human nature is like Passion, and desires its good things now: it requires an extra inducement to act like Patience and wait for its good things till a future time. Capital is the fund of wealth; income is the extra inducement which proves sufficient to make a man use his hoard as capital. It is not necessary to consider now whether he ought to be paid for doing so, or whether time is one of the gifts of God for which no man has a right to charge. It may be enough to say on this matter that he does not charge for time, but by time and in terms of time for the use of his capital. The question of right and wrong will be touched on below, and all that has to be considered here is the practical matter; men will not, as a matter of fact, lend or employ, and so lie out of, their money, unless they have not only satisfactory assurance that their wealth will be restored to them in e.g. a year's time, but also the extra inducement of something more in the future than they have now; not only capital but a year's income. Even in days when the taking of interest was forbidden the justice of this feeling was fully recognised, for it was universally held that to lend on good security, without interest, was a piece of charity, a virtuous act, and one in which some amount of sacrifice was involved.

There are, however, two different ways in which a man may use his capital so as to get an income; he may lend his capital and bargain for interest, or he may employ his capital in expectation of a profit.

1. If he lends his capital, he simply has as a man of business to take account of the borrower, his probable ability to pay interest and to repay the loan. He may not feel sure as to the borrower's ability to do either one or the other, especially if he is lending to a poor man, and in this case (*a*) he will require security of some sort before he makes the loan; or he may feel doubts about the borrower's honesty, and his willingness to pay when he can, and in this case also he will require security. When the Templars in France agreed to pay King John a sum of money in England in silver, they first made him pay an equal sum of gold into the Temple treasury at Paris. The excellent Bricstam, who made gratuitous loans to the needy, was obliged to take pledges from them because they were so very careless about paying him back. The man who is wealthy can borrow easily, because he has property he can pledge; and the wealthy man with a good character can get loans on very easy terms indeed.

(*b*) In modern times we find that great bodies like municipalities and states, which have powers of levying taxes
and can borrow on the security of the rates, are able to
borrow most easily, and as they are anxious to continue to
do so, they are careful to keep a good character for the
punctual payment of interest. So, too, wealthy landowners
can borrow on mortgages, and great railway companies find
that the easiest way of obtaining capital is by issuing deben-
tures and borrowing on the security of the property of the
company as a going concern; and hence there is a very
large amount of capital which is invested in this form, and
lent on more or less satisfactory security.

One curious consequence is that since public bodies are
so wealthy and so punctual in payment they can borrow on
particularly easy terms. Hence the Government can obtain
the use and control of additional capital more easily than any
one else—at 2¾ per cent. Similarly, big companies and
wealthy firms can borrow more, and more easily than smaller
ones; they can get the command of additional capital on
easier terms. This gives the large employers a great advantage over small ones in the struggle for existence, and it gives
public bodies a distinct advantage over companies in carrying on any undertaking. So far as management goes, public
bodies are apt to be extravagant; but so far as the terms on
which they obtain the use of capital are concerned, they can
do it exceedingly cheaply. One of the incentives for the
municipalisation of gas works and water supply lies in the
fact that the town can procure the necessary capital on easy
terms.   .

(*c*) It is of course private capital still; the borrower
merely has the use of it, and will have to repay it; but so
long as there are many private individuals with funds of
wealth, the Government or local bodies can procure capital
on easy terms, and use it as if it were their own. There is
on every side a tendency to rely in business on the use of borrowed capital, as we shall see below. Borrowing is the easiest
way to get capital; and lending is with many capitalists,
especially trustees, a favourite form of employing money. It

is so very free from risks; the capitalist lends his capital, he does not hire it out as the landlord hires out a farm or a house. The house will be somewhat deteriorated—he gets it back subject to reasonable wear and tear; so too with the farm and its buildings. ' But the capitalist does not hire out a piece of property expecting to get back the same piece of property slightly worn but unimpaired; he lends a certain amount of value expecting to get back the same amount of value when the loan is repaid; he bargains himself out of risks so far as the diminution of his principal is concerned. Many capitalists, too, like to know what they can count upon in the way of income; they are willing to accept a very moderate return for their capital, if they are sure to get it regularly and to be spared the discomforts which arise from the difficulty of adapting their mode of living to a fluctuating income. It is, therefore, in many ways a favourite mode of employing money. The capitalist does not much trouble himself about the reasons why any government or company or individual wishes to borrow, or what use is made of the capital he lends; it is usually enough for him if he sees his way to get repaid his principal without depreciation, and to obtain an annual return that he can count upon with regularity in the form of interest.

2. There are other capitalists who employ their money in the expectation of profit; they may get considerably larger sums than those who are contented with interest, but they have also to undertake risks which the lender bargains himself out of. There is the risk of depreciation of the capital itself, and the uncertainty as to the amount of return that will accrue in any given period. It may be large or it may be small, or it may be nil; but whatever it is, it is pretty sure to vary, and not to continue steady for a considerable period as interest does. It is thus a very different thing from interest; the two are often, though not necessarily, connected, as the lender in nine cases out of ten is able to get his interest because the borrower has used the capital lent him so as to earn a profit. Profit often lies behind interest: but the bargain for interest is different in many ways, from the

enterprise of those who are looking for profits, and the two
kinds of employment for money are perfectly distinct.

There are two different ways in which the possibility
of profit seems to arise; though they are often combined
together, still they may be stated apart. One lies in the
improvement of natural processes, the other lies in the
employment of natural forces so as to save time; the great
difference between agricultural and industrial or commercial
pursuits seems to rest on this distinction. Of course, as Mill
pointed out, all human labour consists in putting things in
such places as to bring natural forces to bear on materials
furnished by nature; but in some cases we cannot hurry
natural processes, we cannot get two wheat harvests in one
year off the same land in England. The arable farmer cannot
turn his capital over more than once a year. But in commerce and manufactures capital may be so used as to save
time; every application of natural forces which brings about
a saving of time is a gain to the public, and to the capitalists
who cater for the public, as they may turn their capital over
many times in the year.

(*a*) The art of the farmer is to combine natural processes
in the most profitable manner. The natural process which
results in the production of wheat will exhaust the soil; he
can stimulate it by bringing into play the natural process of
fertilisation which is effected by manures, or he may give
scope for the natural process of recuperation which takes
place when he follows a rotation of crops or lays down a field
for pasture. By high farming he will get more produce out
of the land in the course of the year; but he will not get a
corn crop ripened more than once a year. He improves the
production, but he does not make the process of production
more rapid.

(*b*) On the other hand the whole work of the capitalist,
manufacturer, or merchant consists in making the process
more rapid. The single labourer can make 1000 pins by himself and with tools he can handle himself; but he will make
1000 pins in less time by the division of labour which capital
facilitates, and by the introduction of machinery which

capital provides. Manufacturing industry has been so often taken as the typical form of capitalist production that economists are inclined to treat this as a sufficient account of the function that it provides intermediate products, and thus brings to bear all sorts of forces that can be made to facilitate or to hasten production.

The capitalist with a considerable business connexion can cater for distant markets, and can therefore manufacture on a larger scale; he is therefore able to employ more hands than the man who has only a small shop; he can arrange to have the division of labour carried further, and this is a great saving of time. More can be done by dividing the labour and assigning each man a special task in which he attains a high degree of skill. Every business man would like to enlarge the scale on which his business is done, but he is limited by his capital; he must have so much wealth invested in materials and so much in buildings and tools, so much money to pay his labourers wages, and he cannot work on a larger scale without more capital to use in one or other, perhaps in all these directions. Capital is a requisite of production in modern society, where manufacture is carried on for sale and with distinct reference to the size of the market, and without it the division of labour cannot be introduced or carried further.

It is equally clear that the use of machinery gives a saving of time; it enables the man who has a machine to produce a greater quantity in a given time, or each article produced involves less expenditure of time. If he can make 300 pairs of boots instead of 100 in the course of a year, with the use of a machine, the machine saves two years of time. Tools are means of saving time, and the better the tools are the more quickly can a piece of work be done. By the intervention of capital there are improved facilities given for natural processes or there is a saving of time in the production of goods, and this is the source from which the profit comes.

II. The Flow of Capital and the Machinery of Investment.

1. It is already clear that the differences between human beings are such that some capitalists may prefer to lend and obtain interest, while others invest in the hope of getting a profit. There is somewhat less of fluidity in capital invested than in capital lent; it may in many cases be very much harder to realise. In the investments and securities which are transferred on the Stock Exchange, and the shares of which are quoted from day to day at a market price, there are differences which render some attractive to one class of inventors and some to another.

a. One man may like a large income and take the chances of ultimate loss in the belief that he will be able to realise before any serious mischief occurs. High profits are sure to attract capital to any particular industry. It has already been pointed out that secured high profits give the opportunity of forming capital fast; it is also true that high profits in any employment attract a flow of capital to that employment. Those who are in the trade already can borrow easily, and others think that this trade is a promising field for enterprise and start in it.

b. But it is also true that some men will invest in a particular stock not because the dividend is high—there may be no dividend at all—but because the price is low, i. e. because they expect that in a few months or years the enterprise will pay or pay better. Anything is worth buying if you can get it cheap. And the man who has faith in some project may be induced to invest in it largely when the price is low. If the industry revives, the rate of profit will be good, and he can realise his capital at a much higher figure.

The same sort of thing may be seen in other cases; during a period of great depression in the cotton trade in Lancashire it was noticeable that new mills were rising in all directions even when the existing ones were running half time. Those who believed that the trade would recover saw that a time of general depression was one when prices of all sorts were low, when building could be done on very easy terms, when engineers were ready to supply machinery at little over cost price, and so forth. It therefore became possible to build and fit mills with all the newest improvements on specially advantageous terms, and the men who had faith in the future of the industry took the opportunity of bad times to invest more largely than before.

There are here two different types of mind; in both cases the 'desire of wealth' is the motive force, but in one case it is the desire of as large an income as possible now, in the other it is the desire of an improving property. One man invests for the sake of a high return, the other invests in the hope of increasing his capital.

c. Men will be affected in different ways by the possibility of understanding the details of the business in which their money is engaged. Many capitalists unite the actual management of some business with the employment of their capital; they prefer to put their money in a business they themselves understand, as they know more clearly what are the real risks and net profits of the trade. In such cases there are individual tastes and preferences that limit the free flow of capital. The nearness or the distance of the property concerned will affect them, inasmuch as they feel they can get little full information about an enterprise in distant lands; and the uncertainty of the view which may be taken of shareholders' or bondholders' rights by foreign courts will also prevent capitalists from looking eagerly at such investments. But, after all, there are always men who will take the risk if they see a high profit, or fancy they can buy cheap; there is a slight barrier, but a very slight one, to the free flow of English capital to the most distant places and the least settled territories. The capitalist is indifferent to the direction in which he invests so long as he is likely to be able to control, or at least to realise, his principal and to secure a return as income.

2. There exists in the present day a very elaborate machinery by which capital is transferred from one employment to another.

(*a*) Capital when newly formed probably shows itself

in the form of a large credit in the owner's account at
his banker's, and while it is lying there it is available for
temporary advances to those who need it. The banker is a
money-lender on a large scale, and the man who wishes to
borrow capital in order to extend his business, or to tide over
a temporary emergency, can do it most easily through his
banker. It has been already seen that the forms of credit
are convenient aids to the formation of capital, and they
certainly afford every facility for the transfer of capital into
the hands of those who are able to use it. If the balances of
customers with their bankers are large, the bankers will be
able to lend on easier terms ; everybody who sees a prospect
of driving his trade will be able to procure the necessary
capital with unusual ease, and trade will be stimulated everywhere.

(*b*) It is also through the banks and bill-brokers that capital
is transferred to foreign lands. If a railway is being built in
Turkey by English capital, wealth will be transmitted in the
form of English exports to Turkey for which no equivalent in
goods will be brought here; the equivalent is being converted into a railway on Turkish soil; similarly when the
railway is made and the profits or interest are being transmitted to the English shareholders, there will be imports of
Turkish goods into England for which no equivalent in goods
is exported. The value of the capital and the value of the
interest are alike represented by bills, and these bills can be
met in many cases by goods which are transferred in the
course of trade without the export and import of large sums
of money. But it is unnecessary to dwell here on the delicate mechanism which has been so well described by authorities like Mr. Bagehot and Mr. Rae.

(*c*) The whole Stock Exchange exists for the purpose of
enabling capitalists to transfer their capital from one investment to another. As an institution it has many critics ;
much of the business that is done upon it is of a highly
speculative character, and those who gamble may be led
into other vices. But, apart from its bearing on individual
character, it is said that many of the dealings on the Stock

Exchange are of an unsocial character. In other transactions, it is said, each of the parties to an exchange gains, and there is therefore a social advantage from the fact that the exchange takes place; but on the Stock Exchange one man's success is simply and directly another man's loss, and each man gains at somebody else's expense, and therefore as an economic institution it is thoroughly bad. We are not concerned at present with the morality of the Stock Exchange, or the limits of legitimate speculation, but simply with the practical question of its actual working and its effects on the administration of capital.

It may be noticed in passing that the statement that one man's gain is another man's loss is only true in degree; that in so far as men have different motives in investing, what has ceased to be a desirable property for one man may have come to be a desirable property for another, and each by exchanging may obtain something that they want more than the thing they had. But after all the social advantage of the Stock Exchange does not accrue from the combined gains of individual dealers; it arises from the fact that by their dealings—speculative dealings, it may be—they keep the market going for capital, so that the man who desires to invest can easily get the sort of thing he wants. If there were no Stock Exchange with speculative transactions there would be far less facility for the transfer of capital, and far greater difficulty in finding the necessary means for floating new enterprises.

3. It is undoubtedly an enormous social advantage of a practical character that there should be easy means of transferring capital to those persons or places who can make it most serviceable, and who are therefore best able to pay for it. It is an immense practical benefit that progress should not be hampered, but that the enterprising man should be able to float some ingenious project. But while these advantages are fully recognised, and while they appear to outweigh any minor evils that accompany them, it is yet worth while to remember that there are accompanying disadvantages of a practical kind.

(*a*) In the first place, the great facilities for floating well-planned enterprises also render it more easy to float ill-considered and fraudulent enterprises; they pave the way for the most profitable employment of capital, but they also lead to a very great waste and destruction of capital—a matter which need only be mentioned here as it is examined at greater length below.

(*b*) In the second place, the very fluidity of capital appears to intensify the great industrial evil of the present day; this lies in the extraordinary fluctuations of trade. One year men will be working many hours a day at over-time wages, and in the next year things are slack; they work half time or get paid off altogether. Temporary high profits in any trade lead to the rapid formation of companies to carry on this kind of business, and the rapid production which ensues leads to a glut and to depression. So, at least, it is said; how far this mischievous tendency has really occurred to any considerable extent, how far it is connected with the Stock Exchange, and not with the formation of small companies, which never come to be quoted at all beyond the localities where they are formed, are matters on which it is impossible for an outsider to form an opinion. Similarly, it is not easy to say how far the Stock Exchange as an institution is responsible for the waste of capital; or how far its regulations have checked such frightful waste of capital as occurred in the days of the South Sea Bubble. It may be enough to say that the practical advantage of giving great fluidity to capital, and of bringing it to bear in those regions where it can work more effectively, is very great; and the onus of proof appears to lie with those who believe that this social gain is more than counterbalanced by accompanying evils.

III.　The Increase of Borrowing and its Effects.

So far we have considered the investment of capital and the machinery by which it is accomplished. We have tried to break up the 'desire of wealth' into its different elements, and to show how the play of distinct motives affects the investment of capital in various ways. The most complete explanation we can hope for is obtained when we have found the spring of action which influences the owner to prefer one mode of employing capital to another. There seems to be reason to believe that the convenience of the public and of many who possess capital is best served when the owner does not employ it himself but lends it to Government or to companies; and that the practice of borrowing capital is on the increase. In closing this chapter it is worth while to point out that the practical issues we have been considering seem to show that tendencies are actually at work in the present day which have a very close connexion with some of the social problems to which allusion has already been made, and with some of the ethical questions which will be discussed below. At the risk of some iteration, which may appear unnecessary, it is worth while to indicate here how they arise.

1. The large investments of capital in foreign lands form international connexions, and give rise to cross-relationships; they do something to break down the strong nationalism of old days. The possession of capital abroad gives English citizens a stake in the prosperity of other countries; they no longer regard them as mere rivals. Nor is this effect confined to owners of capital only; for the antagonism to capital in distant lands rouses a sense of sympathy in the labouring classes everywhere, and international agitation becomes possible. One of the great obstacles to socialism has lain in the existence of national rivalries and jealousies, and the more those jealousies fall into the background the less impossible does some sort of international economic organisation appear. The opinion has been already expressed that though national differences are less important economically than they were, they are still so real that it is absurd to leave them out of account, even in regard to economic affairs. But though this seems to be true, it is yet noticeable that they are of less economic importance and of decreasing importance. Capital appears to be undermining one of the great obstacles to socialism.

2. The greatly increased facilities for the practice of borrowing capital, and the favour which this practice finds both with wealthy borrowers and with lenders who like a regular income, raise very important questions as to the personal responsibilities of the rich. The lender lets the capital entirely out of his control, and feels no practical concern in the use that is made of it; this in a lesser degree is true of those who have shares in the companies which are now so easily formed under the Limited Liability Companies Acts. And hence the moral question is coming more and more to the front. How far are capitalists really responsible for the manner in which borrowers use their capital, or for the manner in which the business is done by a company in which they have shares, while they exercise no appreciable influence on the management? To this subject we must return in a subsequent chapter.

CHAPTER VIII.

Capital in Action.

I. The Services of Capital to the Public.

It needs no demonstration to show after what has been stated above that capital renders great services to the public. In so far as it is employed in enterprises it is used for facilitating natural operations and saving time in the production of useful goods, i. e. of things people wish to use. It thus confers benefits on the public, for it supplies them with the goods they wish in greater quantities or with more rapidity than could otherwise be the case. Much of the capital that is lent is also used in this way so as to bring about public advantage; the money that is lent to industrial or commercial companies, or used by Government for public works, is used for the general advantage. In some cases a borrower may obtain money which he merely squanders, and from which no public advantage accrues, but on the whole it may be said that the world or the nation or some smaller portion of the public is greatly the better in all sorts of material welfare because of the intervention of capital.

1. This is the side of the matter that has been observed by economists of the Manchester School. Senior and others speak with the highest enthusiasm of the national and communal advantages which arise through the action of men who save and employ capital. They are apparently regarded as the greatest civic benefactors; they seem to be possessed, as Cato said, with an almost divine virtue; for it could hardly be doubted that men who conferred such benefits on society

were possessed of excellent qualities, and their thrift and
abstinence were universally extolled. It cannot be denied
that the ordinary millionaire modestly concealed these virtues
under a sufficiently luxurious exterior, and did not appear
unto men to fast. The absurdity of this laudation is sufficiently obvious in àny case; whether out of virtue or of self-
interest, the great capitalists had their reward. But there is
a danger lest the reaction against these absurd expressions
should lead us into an opposite blunder and make us forget
that, though the capitalist becomes rich, he does not become
rich at the expense of the public, but only because his enterprise and skill confer a real benefit on the public. If he
makes a railway which no one wants and nobody uses, he
does not become rich, but contrariwise loses his capital. His
chance of becoming rich lies in successfully catering for the
public, and it is just because the public are first served and
well served that he gets an addition to his wealth. Some
exceptions to this may occur in the case of monopolies, but
it is true on the whole. Capital does render a great service
to the public.

2. But because capital affords an advantage to the public,
in so far as it supplies consumers more easily, it does not
follow, as more recent economists have assumed, that capital
affords a great advantage to the labourer who produces.
Whether it does or does not depends very much on his point
of view. It may save his time, and it is then an advantage
to the man who works by the piece; but it is not so clearly
a gain to the man who works by the hour and who does not
find his time fully occupied. To talk of the labourer obtaining the use of capital on easy terms is to talk as if capital
were the labourer's servant, whereas it is often his master.
It is to assume a complete solidarity of interest between all
those engaged in the process of production; there may be
this harmony over any period of years, but there is apparent
divergence of interest from day to day and week to week.
Conditions which favour the consumer need not necessarily
favour the producer; or how could there be an outcry for
protective tariffs and fair trade and sugar bounties? Because

the introduction of machinery or the investment of capital renders a service to the public, it does not necessarily render a service to the labourer too. It may save him drudgery by enabling the work to be done more quickly and with less exertion ; indeed it may enable his employer to dispense with his services altogether. There is pure irony in saying of a man who has all his time on his hands and can earn nothing, that capital has rendered him the service of giving him a perpetual holiday.

Hence it cannot be a matter of surprise that some socialists have been inclined to seize on this side of the action of capital. They look at capital not primarily in its bearing on the public as consumers, or not at all in this aspect. They lay stress on the action of capital on the labourers as producers, and they think that there is a tendency on the part of capital to displace the labourer, to diminish his opportunities of employment, and to lessen the returns he receives for his work. To such men the talk about the services rendered to the labourer by capital seems as absurd as the old panegyrics on the thrift and abstinence of the capitalist. They contend, on the contrary, that the growth of capital has coincided with the depression of the artisan, and that capital is not the servant but the enemy of the labourer. There is a sufficiently violent conflict of opinion here, and it will need some pains to enable us to discriminate how far the various antagonists are in the right.

3. As to the general assertion that capital does render great services to the public—whether we mean the world, or the nation, or some smaller community,—there can be little doubt that capital enables us to have greater quantities of goods and to have goods from greater distances. If we may be sure that national welfare and progress is a good thing, then we may be also assured that what renders that progress more easy and rapid is also a good thing. (*a*) It is perfectly true that men lived and worked, and lived well and worked well, when little or no capital was employed in industry. Great works were undertaken slowly, and big buildings erected with the savings that could be afforded from each year's crops,

without the accumulation of any store; but this was not always the best way to do the work. In many cases there is a loss that can be definitely assessed in money when some work is allowed to drag on instead of being brought to a conclusion as fast as may be; but the disadvantage of slow and tedious work can be exhibited from another point of view. We are apt to cry out in the present day about the whirl and bustle of life, and to look back with regrets to times when there was less hurry and more calm; and for self-development in culture and the maintenance of high ideals some retreat from the bustle of life may serve as a necessary self-discipline which may ultimately react most favourably on society. But in so far as the enjoyment of material goods is to be regarded as an important element in human welfare the greater rapidity of life is a distinct gain.

Because the world moves faster each man has during his life a greater number and variety of things at his command. He can command and use the products of distant lands, because they are brought so fast and so easily; he can spend a holiday in another county, or even in another country, because of the rapidity of travelling. To have work done quickly is a good thing, because we are able to enjoy the results of it sooner. There is a royal satisfaction in founding a palace to perpetuate the name of a conqueror, but there is also a satisfaction in finishing the palace before you die, so as to be able to live in it. Akbar and others built palaces which they never lived to complete, and as their successors did not care to occupy another man's foundation, they have even failed to obtain the posthumous fame they hoped for. Many Benedictine Abbeys took generations to complete, but the Cistercians worked more rapidly because they procured capital from the Jews in order to build their great churches; they wished to complete them in less time than was otherwise required. It is perfectly true that all sorts of magnificent things can be accomplished without capital, and there are some things, like the growth of a forest of oaks, which capital can do very little to hasten; but those who build a big church may like to have it to use before they die, and the benefit which capital confers is shown in their being able to use it sooner.

b. The contrast betwixt England in the past and the present brings out three great differences as regards the ordinary comfort of life,—the vast expansion of foreign commerce and the opportunity for enjoying foreign products, including corn ; the greater rapidity with which work can be done, and the diminution of risks of utter disaster and impoverishment. Two of these are obviously connected with the use of capital and the services it renders ; the third is largely due to the fact that capital has been formed so largely, and that there is an immense reserve of wealth to fall back upon. The mediaeval burgess had to be content with a wooden house ; he was constantly exposed to risk of fire. Capital enables him to have a better house of less inflammable materials, and some association of capitalists called an Insurance Company relieve him of the risks of being burnt out of all his property. It has needed great capitals and large expenditure to diminish the risks of flood in the midlands and the fens, and life goes more smoothly as well as more swiftly because capital has been formed and applied in these ways. The greatness of the power of capital has been already illustrated from the growth of the Roman Republic and of the English Empire ; it would be also striking if we could really draw the contrast between the daily life of men in our land in pre-capitalist and in capitalist times.

If we were to compare the past and the present we should find that there were such differences of taste in different ages that no standard is available for us unless we are content with a purely sanatory one, and consider the extent to which anyone could command the things that are requisite for maintaining and prolonging human life. It is pretty clear that a Norman baron, who had no floor to the hall of his castle, no bed to lie on, no plates to eat off, and no glass to drink out of, whose food was sometimes tainted and unwholesome, enjoyed a worse life, from the insurance company point of view, than the modern pauper in a workhouse. Even if we leave out all the risks and uncertainties which come from frequent fighting and occasional famines, we may see that the rich noble fared but badly in old days, and could not count upon the simple comforts which are now found in the poorest houses. It may be that the twelfth century villan was but little worse off in these matters than the twelfth century baron; but in any case we may assume that the poor man was not better provided with material comforts than the rich one. The lot of the labourer to-day is bad enough, but it will still compare most favourably with the condition of those who drudged and toiled as serfs before capital had been formed and came into operation in connexion with English industry. There is much reason to believe that the formation and employment of capital has been the means of conferring benefits on all classes of the community, even when the fullest allowance is made for the mischiefs which have accompanied it.

It is unnecessary to insist on this at greater length, especially as we shall return to it later. We may now turn to consider the nature of the evils which have attended the growth of capital, and which may be seen, partly in connexion with social organisations, and partly in their bearing on individuals.

II. The Destruction of simpler Social Organisations.

1. The growth of capital has resulted in breaking down social and economic organisation. There have been and are various types of economic organisation. The simplest is the village, or family group, which is practically self-sufficing, and where the whole industry of each of the inhabitants can be fitted in so as to subserve the general requirements. There is a village weaver who exercises a traditional art and weaves the necessary clothes for all the inhabitants. But a time is sure to come when the isolated, self-sufficing village is drawn into the circle of trade. The villagers have the opportunity of buying cloth, made with the help of capital, and brought to their doors by the help of capital, and they find that it suits them better than the cloth

supplied by the village weaver. His trade is ruined, his loom is left idle, and the village has ceased to be a self-sufficing economic organisation; it is dependent on trade, perhaps on trade with a distant country, for its supply of cloths. The old village life, with its simplicity and its self-centred neighbourliness, has suffered a serious inroad; it no longer forms a little world of its own, well-ordered and content; it becomes a fragment of a great, struggling, and competing world.

2. Or again, to take another type of economic organism, we may have a city, in which the whole of the trade and industry was regulated for the good of the town and by means of an elaborate system of gilds. There is, we may suppose, a tanning gild who make leather; but when capitalists who manufacture leather in places that are specially fitted for the trade bring leather from a distance, it may easily be that they will undersell the local tanners and destroy their organisation. And in this there is serious loss. It was much easier to supervise the quality of goods when the producer and consumer lived in close connexion, and any well-founded complaint could be the subject of immediate investigation. The mere fact that the supply comes from a distance renders it very much harder for the consumer to get a sufficient guarantee of the quality of the wares, while it also makes it harder for the producer to adapt his output to the requirements of the case. The intervention of capitalist traders and capitalist producers seems to have done much to break down the old municipal regulation of trade and municipal *esprit de corps*. Several of the flourishing towns of the fourteenth century, in each of which a large variety of crafts had been represented, only managed to survive in the seventeenth century because they had succeeded in becoming the centre of a special branch of industry which was organised by capitalists for the supply of a large area.

3. It is thus that the power of capital has broken down the simpler types of economic organism, and, as has been stated above, there is some reason to believe that the power of capital is breaking down the national organisation of industry

and commerce. Nor when we fix our attention on the better sides of the institutions that have gone is it altogether easy to reconcile ourselves to the loss of the simple village life, or the strong *esprit de corps* that created the civic glories of which such meagre vestiges survive. We may look back on them and admire ; but we would also do well to consider the cost which would have been involved in order that these institutions, which at any rate look so well from a distance, might be retained. Industrial organisation requires conditions that are practically fixed, for changes may put the machinery out of gearing ; any little variation will set the industrial organism wrong, however beneficial the ultimate results of the change may be. Village life could only have been preserved by forbidding all opportunities for intercourse with other peoples, as so many of these villages have done and do. The maintenance of the old town life could only have been secured by checking the new development of industry and commerce, as so many towns tried to do. These early forms could only have been retained at the cost of sacrificing all further progress. We cannot wish that the world were all made up of village communities, with no greater possibilities of cultivation than they possess ; or that it should have stayed on the level of the life in mediaeval towns with their narrow jealousies and bitter disputes. Human progress has been a good to mankind, though at each stage there has been a real sacrifice. Each period of transition has involved some elements of loss, but the gain of greater command over the means of life could not be secured without some measure of loss. We cannot make sure of retaining the good in the institutions of any period, unless we can so exclude change as to interfere most seriously with the possibility of any farther progress.

Objection has already been taken to the schemes of those who desire more complete organisation of industry, from the difficulty of selecting the best type of organisation to adopt (p. 64). But the facts which have just been noted indicate another difficulty, for we cannot hope under any circumstances for a completely self-adjusting organisation. Might we not have reason to dread that a nationalised industry could only be maintained in working order if the elements of change, and therefore of progress, were excluded? It is at least important that any one who proposes the thorough-going national organisation of industry and commerce should be clear that his scheme not merely allows for organising things as they are, or for organising things as they may be when human powers are greater than they are now, but that it is one which is so devised that it will neither offer serious obstacle to future progress nor be itself unable to stand the strain of the transition.

III. The Decreased Importance of the Labourer.

1. The action of capital has now to be considered as it affects the individual prejudicially. The most obvious illustration of this occurs in the introduction of machinery; it is generally recognised that the rapid substitution of machine production for production by hand is likely to diminish the labourer's opportunities of employment, for a time at any rate, and thus to injure him in his capacity as a producer. Stated in general terms, it may be said that machinery renders the labourer a less important factor in production. If machines are introduced into a department of industry which has been previously carried on by hand, and by hand alone, then the man is no longer the only active force in production. By means of machinery other natural forces are introduced to do part of the work which has hitherto been done by human muscles alone, and labour is no longer the sole or even the principal agent employed. More work is done, and probably more gain accrues by the change, but the labourer who formerly did all the work, and therefore got the full reward, now only does a part of the work and therefore only gets a part of the reward. He may in time find that the pay he gets for doing a part in a great deal of work is as large as the pay he formerly got for doing the whole in a smaller amount of production, or he may not. But in any case there is a relative depression in his position

as a producer because he is a less important factor in the process of production.

2. The half century which saw the great introduction of machinery into the textile trades furnished numberless illustrations of the injurious effects which may follow from such a change. In the days before machine industry was introduced, the skilled labourer was sought after as the one means of introducing or perpetuating a trade. Parliament would not allow English woollen weavers to migrate to Ireland, and sought to prevent English citizens from seeking employment abroad; and if skilled workmen, the men who practised the art and understood the secrets of the trade, abounded here, the trade could hardly be transplanted elsewhere. But with the introduction of machinery the skill of the workman came to be of less account; children could be employed to mind machines, and the deftness of the 'manufacturer' ceased to be of primary importance in the trade. He might emigrate or not as he chose, and nobody cared.

(*a*) In the middle of last century it was possible for the weaver to plan his work as he liked; the families engaged in spinning and weaving had often some interest in agriculture, and the two kinds of occupation could be carried on together. But even when the weaver did not get the gain which a bye employment gives he was less pressed; he might have a short day when he saw a chance of a little poaching, and make up for it by a long bout at another time; he was his own master. But with factory industry all this is changed; the machines go on with relentless vigour, doing the regular day's work, beginning at the regular time, and running till the mill closes; each hand must be there and put in full time. There is a remorseless undeviating demand upon the energies of the hands who attend upon machines. Besides this, there has been a tendency to increase the hours of labour; the machine does not need to rest, or, at any rate, needs very brief rests; every idle hour is a loss to the owner of the mill, inasmuch as his machinery is not turning out the work it might do; the more hours he can make it run the more easily does he recoup himself for the outlay expended on the machinery. Human beings, however, need to go from labour to refreshment; but it is quite probable that the owner of the machine will put pressure on the hands who tend it and make them work, not merely the hours they can work and get the needed rest, but hours that leave them no proper intervals for food and sleep, in the hope of reducing the time when the machinery is standing idle. There was a great tendency to lengthen hours unduly, and no means short of the intervention of Parliament in the Factory Acts sufficed to check it.

(*b*) Another very important matter has come to the front since a maximum has been fixed for the hours of labour in factories. There is a desire to make the most of these hours, and therefore to increase the pace at which the machine works, or the demands upon the quickness of the hands. The strain of work may be very greatly increased while the hours of work remain the same; this strain of work cannot be easily measured, or the wear and tear of nervous energy which it involves readily estimated. But it is obvious that in all these ways there is a temptation to treat the machine as the main element in production, and to make it the measure of what the man ought to do, instead of regarding the man as the first consideration and the machine as the instrument which helps him; the machine may be made the primary consideration, and the man may be treated as a mere slave who tends it.

(*c*) The question as to the change in the position of the artisan is often regarded as a matter of wages. To the reward of labour we shall have occasion to return when we come to discuss the remuneration of capital. In the meantime it may be enough to point out that all these tendencies indicate that there is a real depression in the position of the labourer relatively to other factors in production, and that the primary question is not as to changes in the reward of labour, but as to the change in its importance. The artisan's work does not count for so much as it formerly did, and on the face of it one would expect that it would not be paid so well; not because capitalists are greedy and grind the men down, for the force that displaces them is not the selfishness of any master, but the skill which applies a new force to procure the old results more quickly and more cheaply. It is human inventiveness, not in the first instance human greed, that has displaced the labourer. The employer cannot force back the tide which is running; in old days gilds tried to check it and failed; in later times Parliament shrank from attempting the task, and now men see that it is hopeless to keep the trade in its old groove by breaking machines or by violence. The labourer suffers, not because anyone deliberately seeks to grind him down, but because the world has learned to dispense with the services he has been used to render. Blame may attach to those who do not do their best to habituate the labourer to the change, and to make the transition as easy as may be; but even if they are careless about this duty, the change has not been caused by human selfishness, but by the skill that has so adapted physical forces that machine labour has superseded the necessity for so much human labour or such highly skilled human labour. The man who can supply labour is not so much sought after as he was, and can hardly be expected to make such good terms.

There can, I think, be little doubt however that at the time of the industrial revolution not only was there a diminution of the relative importance of labour as a factor in production, but that the labourer began to suffer greatly as to the length of his hours and the intensity of work, not to speak of the rate at which it was rewarded. Granting then that he became of less importance than formerly, and that his welfare was seriously injured by the changed condition of his work, was this in any sense a necessary result, and one that always attends the operation of capital? Is there an iron law according to which capital, while introducing improvement in production, necessarily grinds down labour not merely to a less important position as an economic factor, but to a lower level of material welfare?

It appears to me that there have sometimes been social

conditions in which increasing power of capital was necessarily prejudicial to the labourer, but that there are other social conditions in which no such injurious results occur. The law may have hypothetical validity under certain assumed conditions, but it is a law which only describes the action of capital in so far as these conditions hold good.

IV. Slave Labour in Rome and English Labour.

1. Allusion has already been made to the condition of the Roman Republic at the time when capital was the supreme power, and we have ample evidence as to the view which was commonly taken of labour in those days. Labour was performed by slaves, who were viewed simply and solely as labouring machines. Their lot was degraded, and they were deliberately kept in a state of degradation so that they should be less likely to join in revolt. The servile wars had given the Romans a terrible warning, and they acted on it by drawing the bands most closely on the thralls. The slave was simply a human possession, to be used in such fashion that the greatest possible amount of work should be got out of him in a given time. There was no pretence of recognising any human ties, or any obligation to the slave; he was regarded not so much even as a domesticated animal, but rather as an imperfectly tamed and savage beast that could only be controlled by being kept under. The virtuous Cato, as Plutarch describes him, in his later years 'never failed, as soon as dinner was over, to correct with leathern thongs such of his slaves as had not given due attendance, or had suffered anything to be spoiled. He contrived means to raise quarrels among his servants, and to keep them ever at variance, ever suspecting and fearing some bad consequences from their unanimity.' This period of frugal citizen life was afterwards thought of as a time when the slaves were comparatively well off, and enjoyed an amount of consideration which was never shown them on the large estates of the great land-owners of later times. 'In these times they treated their slaves with great moderation, and this was natural, because

they worked and even ate with them.' But the fact that he shared their labours and their food did not kindle any sympathy in the mind of the frugal citizen. As he weeded his stock of cattle from time to time, so Cato recommended the householder ' to sell such of his slaves as are old and infirm, and everything else that is old and useless,' an observation which moved the indignation of Plutarch, who thought it indicated a mean and ungenerous spirit. Unfortunately it seems to be fairly representative of the ordinary habit; and despite the kindness which was lavished on favourite slaves, or the responsible position which diligent and faithful slaves might enjoy, there can be little doubt that the mere labourer was simply treated as an absolute chattel. The man who sent a valuable slave into a fever-smitten region was held to be foolish in risking his own property when he might have hired a labourer for the purpose; but the old and worn-out slave was a useless property for whom no regard could be shown. The writings of Cato and Varro give us the impression that it was the recognised system of good estate management to get all possible work out of the slaves, and to keep them completely cowed and broken in spirit. We cannot doubt that in such a state of society the iron law would have had free play. Any invention which rendered labour less important would have resulted in a greater carelessness of slave life, and a more reckless assertion of the powers of the master.

But even with all the evils of the present day, the misery caused by the sweating system and all else, there is at least an important difference. The unhappy condition of the labourer to-day is regarded as an evil; it is not maintained as the necessary means of carrying on the work that has to be done. There may be some hypocrisy in the commiseration that is expressed; but it is at least a tribute which hypocrisy pays, and there is a public feeling which demands the tribute. In Rome there was none.

2. (*a*) In England in the present day labourers are free, and many of them have the rights of a citizen; none are the absolute chattels of a master. And hence the worst features

of Roman slavery are not known; there is no deliberate effort to keep the labourer in a state of mental and moral degradation. On the other hand, both Church and State devote much effort to educate and improve him. The whole of the Home Mission work, which takes so many forms, and which is largely maintained by the charity of the rich; the whole of the efforts to diffuse and improve primary education, which have placed such a burden on the taxpayers and the ratepayers—a burden that is for the most part willingly borne, and is voluntarily increased by large donations,—marks the difference between the English and the Roman era of capital.

(*b*) Again, this personal freedom introduces another safeguard in the fluidity of labour. The man can seek a new master. He may find it hard to get employment, he may have to tramp the country or to emigrate, and in thousands of cases it may be practically impossible for him to have recourse to either expedient. Still the fact that it is an expedient of which many can and do avail themselves rather than be put upon is not to be forgotten; it marks an entirely different condition of society from that which existed in the time of Cato at Rome. The tone of public opinion is in favour of encouraging a man to better himself when he can, and there are numerous philanthropic and Government agencies which are intended to assist him in seeking better employment.

There are many cases too where the master is to some extent in the power of his men. A great business would suffer if the staff were broken up and a new set of hands who did not know the ways of the place were at once introduced. If his shops are at all busy the master dare not face the difficulty of reorganising the whole concern. The very scale on which business is now done gives the workers an extraordinary pull if they use the opportunities they have of acting together.

(*c*) The freedom of the labourer and the fluidity of labour render it difficult to treat the labourer as a mere producing machine and entirely to ignore his character as a human being. And even if there were the will to do so, public opinion is sufficiently awake and sufficiently disinterested to be able to exercise a very real influence. The commercial interest was, as has been noted above, absolutely supreme in republican Rome; and there was no philanthropic side from which a practical protest was likely to be raised against the maltreatment of the slave. In England at the present time the power of public opinion is constantly felt as protesting against gross and marked evils that attract attention. It is a somewhat spasmodic and fitful influence, easily roused and easily appeased; it is not very discriminating, perhaps, but it certainly is a very considerable power when it is brought to bear, as the story of the Dockers' Strike shows clearly.

So far public opinion has made itself felt as a negative influence. It is roused by this or that wrong, the popular imagination is affected by great suffering and responds to such appeals; but it has never been able to devise an effective scheme of what ought to be. The nearest approach has been in the successive Factory Acts which have limited the hours of labour; they have laid down the limits of the working day in a great number of industries, and the principle is being applied more and more widely, so that the agitation for a uniform eight hours day makes itself distinctly heard and felt as a political power. How far a limit of this kind is desirable, and how far the proposed limit is the right one, it is unnecessary to consider here. The point to be noticed is that we have a very distinct effort to assert the supremacy of men as men over the mere mechanism of production, and to insist that work shall be done on the conditions that suit the man, not on the conditions that suit the machine. It is in the assertion of the absolute value of human life that the safeguard lies against the miserable results of the great era of industrial advance. The world is infinitely richer, but it is very little happier; the strain and drudgery of the lives of millions seem to be as great or greater than before, as Mill sadly complained. It is by asserting the worth of individual human life as such, by insisting that the man's hours shall be such that he may do the best work he can and not be worn out before his time, that a remedy may be found. In this way he will perhaps have more leisure than he is likely to spend in an ideal fashion at first, but at least he will have the opportunity of learning to spend his leisure better. The important thing is to secure that the conditions of labour shall be such as are satisfactory for the life of man, and not such as degrade him in mind or body; and when these are secured the reward of labour is not likely to be the subject of much complaint. For, after all, the conditions of work are the main thing; the advocates of shortened hours too often speak as if the main thing were to give a man leisure; but idleness is a miserable ideal for an individual man, and it is a hopeless one for the race. It is good for a man to have work to do and to be able to do it; to have his faculties of mind and body exerted. They have the happiest lot in life who are able to choose the work that interests them, and to do it with hearty enthusiasm for its own sake.

There are many influences at work which tend to confuse public opinion on these matters, to set a low value on human life, and to idealise idleness rather than work; to popularise, in fact, a Pagan rather than a Christian view of life. And whatever may be the other moralising influences at work which shall serve to keep up the tone of public opinion on this matter, there can be no doubt that Christian teaching is a most important factor. There is no other creed which attaches such high importance to the individual life as immortal and undying, and also to the human body as the instrument of redemption. There is no other religious system where the duty of work has occupied a foremost place as a personal discipline, as it did in the monastic rule, or as affording the means of exercising charity. Paganism in all its forms attaches so little value to human life that it is ready to sacrifice it, and to justify the degradation of some as expedient for the comfort and culture of others. Paganism has always contemned work as degrading, and idealised a selfish idleness which shut its eyes to the needs and sorrows of others. The more these Pagan conceptions affect our ideal for society and for ourselves now, the less hope is there of making the most of the great opportunities we possess for the permanent welfare of society.

d. The influence of public opinion must not be overlooked, but it is doubtful whether it can exercise an effective control over all the work that is done throughout the country, and see that the conditions under which it is carried on are as satisfactory as may be. The little mediaeval towns found it impossible for one body to supervise all trades; it would be still more difficult for a national parliament to understand or give effect to the best possible regulations for each trade in every part of the country. This point has been already mentioned in connexion with the administration of capital; there is at least equal difficulty in connexion with providing improved conditions for labour, and it is at present unnecessary for the State to attempt it for all trades in all places. Organisations of labourers, to regulate the conditions under which work is done, have accomplished much. Trades Unions are not merely concerned with struggling for higher wages; they endeavour to control all the conditions of labour, to see to the risks to life and limb, the irregularity of employment and so forth, as well as to the rate of reward. Just as there seems to be need for the individual and associated administration of capital in some departments, so it appears probable that the conditions of labour are better seen to by special associations like Trades Unions than they could be by any general body. It may be doubted if the Social Democracy could ever be organised so as to give such effective control of each trade as the Unions now exercise, or to offer such occasional interference and constant criticism as is supplied by the organs of public opinion.

When we fix our attention, not on the miseries of the present day—miseries which are due to many and complicated causes—but on the facts with regard to labour which distinguish English from Roman society, we may see that the political freedom of the labourer, the fluidity of labour, and the force of public opinion and of trade organisations, place the modern artisan in an entirely different position from the Roman slave. He may be badly treated, but he is regarded as a man. How fast or how slowly the same or similar influences may be brought to bear on the unskilled labourer, and on woman's work, we need not pause to speculate. There is all the more reason for hope when we remember how rapidly and effectively these forces have come into play in improving the conditions for the work of the skilled artisan.

3. (*a*) The time of the industrial revolution in England approximated much more closely than might at first sight appear to the conditions of society in republican Rome. Not that there was the same recklessness in regard to the life of the artisans, but chiefly because the institutions which had been intended to protect him and to secure him favourable conditions had ceased to serve any useful purposes and only hampered him instead. At any rate, while there is a contrast between Rome and England in the present day, there is a 'similar contrast between England a century ago and the England of to-day. The artisan, generally speaking, had no voice in the government of the country, and had not the full powers of a free citizen. Fluidity of labour was very seriously hampered by the law of settlement, and, as Adam Smith has pointed out, the Englishman was put at a distinct disadvantage by the obstacles which conspired to prevent his going to seek employment in districts where it might be obtained on more favourable terms. He had none of the security which is given by political freedom and by the fluidity of labour.

(*b*) Besides this it was almost impossible to arouse public opinion on his behalf, for the public were inclined either to trust to the efficacy of the old institutions, or to believe that things would right themselves if the old institutions were swept away. The artisans themselves appear to have been satisfied with the protection the Elizabethan statutes gave them, and only asked to have these statutes carried out, and the Berkshire justices patched up the whole scheme of regulation by using the poor rates to supplement starvation wages by allowances. But the Elizabethan scheme had been devised for a state of technical knowledge, when human

strength and skill were the chief elements in production;
the old rules for apprentices and journeymen had no application to the great factories and the running of machines.
To maintain the old system in its entirety would have been
to check the introduction of machinery and to condemn
English industry to the use of cumbrous and old-fashioned
methods. Thus, when the position of the hand-combers in
the worsted trade was first threatened by Cartwright's invention, petitions were organised and a bill was introduced
into the House of Commons for the purpose of protecting
wool-combers from being injured in their manufacture by
the use of certain machines lately introduced for the combing
of wool. This failed to pass and measures were taken instead
to facilitate the introduction of machinery; the annual saving
it caused was estimated at £40,000 a year in 1798, and English
public opinion would not sanction the prohibition. Neither
those who desired to maintain the old safeguards nor those
who had hopes that the system of natural liberty would ex-
tinguish all wrongs were inclined to listen to the proposals
of Mr. Whitbread, who endeavoured to amend the old system
of regulating wages so as to make it effective for good in
the new circumstances, and to prevent them from falling
below a reasonable minimum.

Further, public opinion was deadened by the fact that there
had been a long period of unusually bad seasons, and then
a period of pressure caused by the exhaustion due to the
long wars. There was general misery both in town and
country; if the artisan suffered greatly, he only seemed to
be bearing his share of the common lot, and public opinion
did not recognise anything distinctive or any special call for
interference in regard to his condition.

(c) While public opinion was thus callous, the sufferers
were themselves unable to give effective expression to the
misfortunes of their condition. Under the Elizabethan
system there had been a great code for the regulation of the
conditions of labour and the reward of labour. Those who
combined to upset the provisions laid down by public
authority were promoting disorder and attacking the whole

social system, and thus conspiracy and combination in regard to the terms on which labour should be done had been stringently prohibited. Such compulsion is of course necessary under some form or other wherever there is a complete system of organisation. If public authority undertakes to make arrangements it cannot allow the grievances of private individuals to be an excuse for actively defying it. But the peculiar evil of the period of industrial revolution was this, that while the public authority no longer fulfilled its economic functions and decided the conditions and terms of labour, the laws which prevented the labourers from combining to attain satisfactory terms for themselves were not repealed. The current political philosophy saw no grievance in this; it was entirely concerned with securing free play for the individual, and the political economy of the day was chiefly occupied in struggling against the restrictions which hampered individual action. It was only by degrees that the world saw that individual action was hampered when the labourer was forbidden to combine with other men to secure his own interests; but during a long period the artisan received no assistance from the law, while it was constantly invoked to prevent him from attempting to protect himself. It thus came about that during this period of transition from the Elizabethan to the philanthropic legislation, the English labourer was temporarily placed in circumstances as regards capital which corresponded more closely with those of the Roman slave than with those of the modern artisan.

(*d*) Bitter as the struggle was then, there is ample evidence that the English labourer was never regarded merely as an untamed beast, to be used as much as might be, and to be rigorously restrained; the English poor law, especially in regard to settlements, added to the evil, but its existence marks a difference between England and Rome at the time when things here were worst. Still, it came about that for practical purposes, so far as his work was concerned, the labourer was treated as a mere instrument of production; neither public opinion nor labour combinations did anything to prevent it, or to assert the importance of conducting industry in such a fashion that the labourer should at least enjoy the old standard of comfort, and also have opportunities of attaining something better.

4. There is however considerable room for difference of opinion in the way the facts of the miserable story of the English operative in the early period of the factory system are interpreted. What is their bearing on the more general questions of the relation of capital and labour? On the one hand it is said that they demonstrate the evil of allowing capital to be owned by private individuals; that private capital oppresses labour whenever it gets the chance, and that there can be no security against the repetition of such evils unless capital is removed from the hands of those who deliberately grind down the labourer for their own advantage. The suggested remedy would therefore lie in handing over the control of capital to public bodies.

On the other hand, it may be urged that the degradation of the labourer was due to causes which lay far deeper than any special method of administering capital. The new application of physical forces to the textile industries made him a less important factor in production, and in whatever way capital had been administered, he could not but be a less important factor than he had been before. In the face of this great change in the economic importance of the labourer public authority was paralysed; it could not enforce the old system, and it could not see how to construct a new one. Even in looking back it is difficult to suggest what could have been done by the most enlightened and public-spirited legislature in order to diminish the evils that were then dimly understood. This at least may be said,—that the existence of public regulation and authoritative arrangements for industry which could not be enforced, was one very obvious reason for the misery. It shows that if a national system of industrial organisation breaks down, the very existence of the *débris* of that system delays the application of a remedy. The misery which accompanied the breakdown of the old industrial system is not more conclusive of the mischief wrought by capital in private hands, than it is of the inability of public authorities to adapt their arrangements to new economic conditions. It gives us no reason to hope for immunity from such disaster by substituting one method of administration for the other.

5. There would be more interest in looking, not at the suggested safeguards against a recurrence of the evil, but at the forces which have come into play to remedy it; they have improved the status of the artisan so remarkably, by giving full political freedom, greater fluidity of labour, and more opportunity of supporting his claims by means of public opinion and by his own associations. These remedies must be sought, not in any external conditions, but in the personal convictions and aspirations which supply the springs of human action. It may surely be hoped that powers which have effected so great a change within our own time will be able to accomplish much in the future, unless their force is exhausted. There are two influences which may be noticed.

(*a*) On the one hand there are the political doctrines which had been formulated in England by Milton, Locke, and Godwin, and which acquired a new force from the triumph which similar opinions obtained in the French Revolution. The Reform Bill, the Chartist agitation, and much else may be regarded as the practical expression of this long literary tradition of political doctrine.

(*b*) There was, however, another movement which affected the upper and middle classes, and which must not be ignored. The evangelical revival had given a considerable impulse to philanthropy; it had called forth action on behalf of African slaves, and it had devoted itself to missions in heathen lands; it did not long continue to ignore the crying needs of sufferers at home. Attempts to diffuse education emanated very largely from men of this type, and the agitation in regard to the Factory Acts was greatly strengthened by the energy of Lord Shaftesbury. These two distinct influences, literary and religious, have sometimes been ranged in opposition to one another, but they have on the whole co-operated to work an extraordinary change. Nor can it be said that either is completely exhausted as practical forces in the present. So long as Woman's Suffrage is a subject of contention the commonplaces of Locke's political theory are not likely to be left to rest in silence ; and if philanthropy is not always wise it certainly is not extinct.

The fact that there has been such a remarkable recovery on the part of the artisan population of status and importance is one that goes far to justify the wisdom of Parliament in refusing to stop the introduction of machinery and the organisation of industry on wholly new lines. Material progress gives the opportunity of gain of every kind, material and moral and intellectual. It is a false policy to check a step in advance, even though that step leads into dark places and troublous times. Just as the maintenance of old organisations was incompatible with progress, so too was the maintenance of the old status of the labourer incompatible with progress. But after all the progress was real, and the proof of it lies in the fashion in which the artisan has recovered, not indeed the precise economic importance that he had in the Elizabethan regime, but a better status as a citizen and greater opportunities as a man than he has ever enjoyed before.

CHAPTER IX.

The Replacement of Capital.

I. The Manner of Replacement.

THERE are considerable differences in regard to the replacement of capital according to the different ways in which it is employed.

1. So far as capital which is lent is concerned the replacement of capital takes place when the loan is repaid. The lender gets his capital back into his own hands, and the transaction is completed. In other cases, as in money lent to the Government, and included in the consolidated debt, there is very little likelihood that the lender will survive to be repaid by the borrower. But he may find some other person who is willing to buy him out and to take his place as a national creditor. He then sells his right to draw $2\frac{3}{4}$ per cent. on a certain sum, and by this means has his capital replaced. The replacement of capital is a very simple matter when it has been lent; for it is supplied as money, and is repaid as money, and the lender has never to consider it in any other form.

2. The replacement of capital engaged in a commercial speculation is also comparatively simple. The picture-dealer buys a certain number of pictures and keeps them; his business connexion enables him to sell them again, and the growing reputation of some artists or the vagaries of public taste may enable him to sell them for much more than he gains. He makes a venture, and his capital is replaced when he sells the wares which he purchased with it, and which he

made up his mind to hold till he saw a chance of getting rid of them advantageously. Here his capital is invested in one particular kind of wares, and it is replaced, after a longer or shorter number of years, and replaced with more or less gain, according as the dealer is successful or not. And capital engaged in trade is all replaced in some such fashion; it is laid out in the purchase of wares, tea or tobacco, or cotton, or cloth, or anything else, and it is replaced when the wares are sold.

(*a*) Whereas in the case of lent capital the replacement takes place when the borrower pays, and the lender has a definite claim upon some one individual, the position of the trading capitalist is quite different. He expects that his capital will be replaced by some individual or individuals from among the public, but he does not know by whom; he may have a pretty shrewd suspicion as to which of various clients is most likely to purchase the goods, but unless he has a contract he has no claim upon any one of them to do so, and he certainly would not refuse a good offer from a new customer. It is thus true to say that the dealer caters for the public, and that his capital is replaced by the public   Inasmuch then as he cannot claim the replacement of his capital by any individual in particular, his trade is due to enterprise; it is a speculation, for he carries it on in the expectation that it will turn out all right. He caters for the wants of the public as he understands them or can forecast them, and he expects that somebody will purchase his goods, and that by thus purchasing the public will replace his capital.

(*b*) When his capital is replaced he can start on another transaction; he can buy a new lot of goods and sell them again so that his capital is again replaced, and every time he completes the process of buying and selling again he turns over his capital. He invests money in goods, and sells the goods for money, and thus turns the whole over. Now it is obvious that he would not undertake the risk of catering for the public unless he expected to be able to sell for a larger sum than that at which he bought. In many cases his ability to do so is due to the fact that he meets the convenience of the

public. He sells in small quantities and near their doors ; he
sells all sorts of different things that they want so that they
do not need to go about from place to place to get their
various requirements. Of course, in so far as he is engaged
in a carrying trade and brings things from a greater or less
distance he may be said to be engaged in a branch of industry and to be putting things where they are wanted.
The justification of such gains, and the possibility of dishonest
gains from trade, will be considered below. In the meantime
it may suffice to say that the trader expects when he turns
over his stock not only to have his capital replaced, but to
have it replaced with a gain ; and unless this expectation is
fulfilled, he cannot and will not think it worth while to
continue to undertake the thankless task of catering for a
public who do not wish to have the things he is ready to
supply.

(*c*) Now it is obvious that the more rapidly he is able to
turn over his stock and to get the accruing gain the larger
will his profits be. The man whose capital is engaged in
arable farming can only turn over his stock once a year ; the
flower-girl will try to turn over her stock once a day. There
may be the greatest difference in the rate at which replacement can take place in different trades. A Bond Street
jeweller cannot in all probability accomplish the feat in one
year, or indeed in several years, while the ordinary haber-
dasher will wish to turn over his stock twice or four times a
year, so as to provide the necessary variety for each season.
But in any case the desire is to turn over as rapidly as may be,
and not to keep on hand a mass of goods which have not
attracted public taste, and which are less likely to find
purchasers at remunerative prices if they are stored still
longer ; hence the sales at enormous sacrifices which force
themselves on our attention at the close of the season. It is
obvious, too, that the system of cash payment is advantageous
to the dealer, because he is able to get his capital replaced
more quickly, and thus either to turn over his stock more
frequently in the course of the year or to do business on a
larger scale.

This is, of course, an object at which he will aim, as in most branches of commerce there is very little additional expense in carrying on the concern on a large scale. If there is profit to be made at all, the more capital is available the larger the sum obtained will be, and it may be secured at the same or even at a better rate. A period of high prices will enable him to expand his trade, as he not only has the opportunity of saving and adding to his own capital, but he can also obtain the use of capital more easily as he has better credit for borrowing. But it is more important to lay the foundations of steady growth. Hence the more a man can force new business connexions, and find purchasers for his goods in different districts or different parts of the world, the more certain can he be of a regular trade, as he is less exposed to the fluctuations which are due to severe local depression. But whether he is dealing on a large scale or a small, the gain accrues when his capital is replaced by purchase. The precise gain he makes each time his capital is replaced must of course be due to the success of his speculation, or more properly to his skill in forecasting the requirements of the public and his success in meeting them. But although his gain comes from a series of transactions, and from turning over his stock in longer or shorter periods, it is convenient for purposes of account to reckon the returns annually, and thus the profit he makes in the course of a year from all his dealings, be they many or few, may be regarded as the income from his capital, and an income which accrues to him from his success in catering for the requirements of the public.

3. There is much greater difficulty about the replacement of capital that is employed in industry; for the manufacturer does not, like the trader, use his money merely to buy certain goods and sell again. The cotton-spinner is engaged in carrying on a process, and he has to keep himself provided with all the things that are requisite for this process. If his business is to be kept going, each part of the process must be organised on a scale which makes it fit in with the other parts of the process, so that the whole undertaking from the

time when the raw material is received till the finished goods are delivered shall be carried on continuously as a going concern. His capital is replaced through the sale of the goods, but his stock-in-trade has to be maintained in all its various parts, so that the complete process may be constantly proceeding.

(*a*) This brings us to consider the parts of which a manufacturer's capital consists at any given time. We shall find it in the simplest form if we consider what the Roman capitalist had to provide who carried on the manufacture of wine. He had, of course, to work the vineyard for the produce, and this was done by gangs of slaves, who were chained as they worked all day, and had no relief from their bonds when they were driven to the miserable underground prison, with its narrow windows, where they passed the night. The owner had of course to supply them with clothes and food; the proper quantities of both are carefully calculated by Cato. He also had to furnish the necessary buildings and instruments for pressing the grapes and manufacturing the wine, and the necessary casks for taking it to market. The whole fund of wealth which was necessary for carrying on the process may be roughly classified in three parts; the materials required, the tools, including the buildings, and the slaves, with their food. In the case of free labour the workers cease to be part of the property, and they are not to be themselves included in the fund of the manufacturer's possessions. But as he needs to be able to procure labour in order that the process in which he is engaged may continue, he has to provide himself with the means of hiring labour with food or with money. His capital will then consist of (1) Materials, (2) Instruments, including buildings, all of which may be named tools, and (3) the means of hiring labour, which we may, for the sake of simplicity, specify Food.

(*b*) There has been a good deal of discussion in recent times as to this old-fashioned way of enumerating the things that make up the capital engaged in industry at any given time. It is obvious that the capital must include *materials*, and materials in every stage of the process, so that the work may go on steadily and continuously, and it is equally obvious that it includes all *tools*—the mill and the plant which is engaged in the manufacture. But there is a difference of opinion about the *food*. It is said that the capitalist does not require to provide for the payment of wages, because the labourers have given him the value of their services before he pays them anything. It is said that in paying wages he does not draw upon his fund, but only restores in another form the value he has already received by the labourers' work.

Now all this is perfectly true, and it has important bearings on many matters connected with the remuneration of capital. It is conclusive against those economists who said that the capitalist deserved remuneration because of the service he did to the labourers in making them an advance of food. He does not make them an advance of food, and therefore he does not deserve to be paid for doing it. As a matter of fact he is not paid for doing it, or for conferring any benefit on the labourers; he is not a salaried philanthropist. He simply gets a gain from the public because he succeeds in catering for the taste of the public and making things which the public wishes to buy. But in order to carry on this process he must have a fund of wealth of different kinds, and part of it must be of a kind with which he can hire labour. If he has not the means of hiring labour the process cannot continue, and even if he has a stock of half-manufactured or of finished goods he cannot hire labour unless he has something the labourer will bargain for—Food or Money. His capital consists of the things that are necessary to carry on the particular process of production in which he is engaged, and he must have command of the means of hiring labor.

The difficulty on this point appears to have arisen because economists have not kept clearly in view the two aspects under which capital may be regarded—its services to the public and its connexion with the labourers who are hired to carry on industrial processes. The capitalist is the middleman; it is he who comes in contact with the public; the labourer has not direct relations with the public, but only through the middleman. The capitalist administers capital so that the whole process of production may go on. He confers a service if you like, not because he makes advances to the labourer, but because he so administers the process of production that there is a saving of time for the public. To manage this he has to take account of the process in all its parts. His success in catering for the public depends on his success in hiring labour and in buying materials. His fund of wealth gives him the means of doing both, and all that he uses to keep the whole process in steady operation is rightly considered his capital.

Nor is the matter altogether trivial, for a clear apprehension of this distinction may help to set other matters in a true light and show us the absurdity of arguing that the men may be fairly regarded as paying the capitalist by allowing him profits for the service he renders to them. We ordinarily say that the capitalist pays his labourers, and so he does; he very seldom pays them in advance, and those economists who thought he always did made a great mistake. The employer does not indeed set aside any fixed and unalterable quantity and call it a wages fund, any more than he sets aside a fixed and unalterable quantity which he calls a materials fund, and refuse to pay more or less. If materials are dear he must pay more if he wants to get them; and if wages are high, he must pay more in order to hire labourers, and he is quite prepared to pay more than he estimated for either one or the other if he sees that he can make it answer. But in any case, the payment made to the labourer for his work passes through the hands of the capitalist and is administered by him. It is true that work is put in before money is paid out, but what the labourer wants is money, and money is paid by the employer.

There appears to be an impression that since valuable work is put in before valuable things are given to the labourer for it, the capitalist's fund of objects of value is not liable to be drawn on for the payment of wages. I cannot feel sure that the precise time of payment affects the matter so greatly; if the employer hires his men on the understanding that they shall have a week's notice, he is always liable for a week's payment beyond the remuneration for work done. The important thing is that they look to him for payment, and that his stock for carrying on the business must include things of the kind that they will accept as payment. The value of the part of his stock which consists of half-manufactured and manufactured goods would be of importance if the business were to be wound up, but it does not afford the means of paying labour and carrying the business on unless the employer uses it as security for obtaining a loan. The increased value of some part of his stock does not enable him to dispense with another part of stock altogether; the process of production cannot be understood if it is all stated in terms of value. The capitalist does not produce abstract objects of value, he produces cotton-yarn or boots, or steam-engines. The whole question is not as to the greater or less value of the capitalist's fund at any time, but as to the precise things of which the capital must consist; it must consist of the objects of value called material in all its stages, and of the objects of value called tools, and of the means of hiring labour, or the process cannot go on. The precise terms of the bargain made with the labourer do not alter the fact that the labourer looks to the capitalist for his pay and that the capitalist must have the means of paying him.

So far as the public is concerned the labourer's share of the work is merged in the process which is carried on by the capitalist; it is only with the capitalist that the public have to deal; he is responsible for the whole affair. It is from his relations to the public and his success in catering for them that the capitalist engaged in industry derives his gain. The whole of the things which are requisite to carry on the process and thus to procure a return are the capital which he uses to get an income. And the corn or money with which he hires the labourers is an essential part of this fund. According to the definition of capital with which we have started there can be no doubt that this element ought to be included. Only if we had limited the application of the term to capital which is employed in industry and defined it as ' wealth which is used to produce more wealth,' would we be justified in excluding from the conception such wealth as is used to reward the labourer who has already produced more wealth. Here once again it may be said that our definition justifies itself, since it accords with the common-sense opinion as to the constituent parts of a mill-owner's capital.

(*c*) When we thus notice the complex nature of the constituent parts of capital employed in industry we see that its replacement, or the turning over of such capital, is a constant process; it involves on the one hand purchases by the public of the products manufactured, and on the other hand the restoration of all the various parts of the producer's stock,—materials, tools, and food,—so that the process of production may continue. But this at least is clear, unless the product is purchased the capitalist finds himself stranded. He has a stock of finished goods which he cannot sell, and till he can sell them he has no means of purchasing more materials, of repairing his tools, or of hiring labour. The sale of his goods is the primary means of replacing his capital in the forms of money, and of thus supplying him with the means of replenishing all the different parts of his stock-in-trade.

It is perhaps worth while to add that the inducement for the manufacturer to extend the scale on which his business is done is even stronger than for the commercial man. The trader in expanding his business can carry on more transactions at presumably the same rate of profit, while the manufacturer can in all probability complete additional transactions at a higher rate of profit. The division of labour can be carried further, there is more scope for the introduction of machinery, and industrial business conducted on a large scale will generally be more profitable than the same business could be if it was less extensive. The supply of manufactured articles at all events can generally be increased at a diminished rate of expense, and hence there is a constant tendency for the manufacturer to expand his business when the opportunity occurs. A period of high prices will give him the opportunity of manufacturing more

largely and extending his connexions as the trader does.
He will make rapid sales and turn over his capital quickly,
and he will strain every nerve to make the utmost use of
the opportunity while it lasts, and supply goods which go
off so quickly and bring in such a satisfactory gain. But the
manufacturer will also seize any chance of so improving his
plant that he can produce more cheaply, and thus be better
able to hold his own if a period of depression should super-
vene. It is thus that success in any industry tends to an
increase of the supply of that kind of manufactured goods
not merely temporarily but for a considerable period, and
if the increased plenty brings it within the reach of a new
or a larger purchasing public, it will give the enlarged trade
a firm and permanent footing.

II. The Rate of Replacement.

1. If lent capital is not replaced, that is to say if the
borrower does not repay his debt, it is eventually wiped out
with more or less of personal inconvenience to the lender
and to the borrower. The history of proceedings in bankruptcy affords numerous illustrations of this state of affairs.
The capital has gone, or most of it has gone, and there is no
use in crying over spilt milk. The immediate result probably
is that someone, be it the lender or be it the borrower, or
both, finds that less wealth passes through his hands and
that he has less power of spending. The bankrupt's credit is
gone and the lender's income is diminished, and neither one
nor the other can afford to be purchasers to the same extent
as formerly.

2. If commercial capital is not replaced, it does not merely
disappear; it continues to be locked up in a stock of goods
which the dealer cannot dispose of. He might indeed force
a sale at a price which would not repay him for his original
outlay, but he has no motive to do this unless the stock is
actually spoiling on his hands; for if he had the money he
would not know how to use it when trade is bad and no
purchasers are forthcoming. He would have to let it 'rot in

the bank,' and he would practically forego all chance of gaining anything by it beyond what is absorbed in his office expenses. Hence it comes about that he is left with the stock on his hands, and he in his turn ceases to be a purchaser, for he has no money with which to enter into new commercial speculations.

3. (*a*) Still further, if the capital employed in industry is not replaced, the process of production must stop or can only continue on a smaller scale. The manufacturer's warehouse is glutted with finished goods which no dealer will purchase, and the manufacturer is thus unable to obtain the money with which to replenish the various kinds of stock he requires. This may be the manufacturer's fault or it may be his misfortune; he may have entirely overestimated the probable demands of the public for whom he caters, or rival manufacturers may have done so and flooded the market with goods; or the public taste may change and leave him with his stock on his hands, and a large portion of his capital locked up in finished goods. And then the process of manufacture may come to a standstill altogether. The manufacturer in this plight will incur a loss by going on, but he incurs a great loss also by reducing his business as he is forced to do. He can neither repair his tools, nor purchase materials, nor pay wages unless he procures money somehow. Probably he will try and reduce every expenditure and keep going somehow; but this must be a serious loss to him. Part of his plant must stand idle, and this is in itself a loss, while the whole will deteriorate from want of care and attention. He can expend but little on materials, and he must reduce the sum he uses in hiring labourers, either by hiring fewer or by paying each man less, or in both ways. There must be a frightful shrinkage in the fund he uses for carrying on the business, and in every way his power of purchasing is greatly diminished. Both the expenditure he himself makes on tools and materials and the expenditure made by his employés on food and clothes is necessarily cut down. The process of production goes on slowly or comes to a stand-still, when the extent of

the shrinkage of capital invested in tools may be measured by noting the small sum which the works and plant will fetch ; though the effects of the loss of that part of capital which he uses to hire labour,—the misery of those who are thrown altogether out of employment, with little hope of finding it again in the depressed condition of trade.—cannot be so readily assessed.

(*b*) As all branches of business are closely interconnected, the disasters which affect one class of society run through the whole ; but the connecting links through which the mischief extends are most noticeable when we consider the replacement, or rather the non-replacement, of capital. The hitch may occur at any point. There may have been a vast amount of wealth accumulated, and this may have been borrowed by a foreign government ; perhaps it ceases to pay interest, and leaves the creditors in doubt about the principal. These creditors, with diminished incomes, purchase less ; so too does the foreign government and its overtaxed subjects. The dealers who usually supply them have their stocks left on their hands, and cannot buy from manufacturers, and they in their turn must diminish the production. When things go as far as this, business of every kind is likely to come to a standstill ; and no one knows where to look for a revival of trade. On some occasion it is a failure of credit and the loss of income on borrowed capital that has reacted upon industry. Or the obstacle which brings about this slackening and stoppage of trade may come from the other side. There may be a succession of bad seasons, so that (if corn cannot be imported) food is dear, and even with the high price many farmers cannot make both ends meet. Agricultural labourers have less to spend, and all labourers have to diminish the amount of their purchases of clothes and food. The capital of the farmer is not replaced, nor that of the manufacturers who supply him and his people, and thus industry receives a check from the diminished consumption.

(*c*) In either case the outward and visible sign of this depressed condition will be found in warehouses packed with goods; there is an apparent superfluity of wealth of every sort, and it appears that the mischief must lie in over-production. The error of capitalists in judging of the real requirements of the public for whom they cater may—like bad seasons or the faithlessness of borrowers—be the first hitch which puts the whole machine out of gearing. But the mischief is always due to some destruction of purchasing power; either the power of purchasing which *rentiers* possess, or labourers or capitalists. Life is a process, and the accumulation of fat, or the distention of some part of the body, shows that the process is going badly. So the economic life of any community is a process, and the material well-being of all is most likely to be secured when that process is going. on smoothly and continuously and rapidly. The check to the process, from whatever side it comes, is sure to lead to gluts, as checking a stream is sure to lead to floods.

Hence the evil can only be removed by something that sets the process going again; the old obstacle may disappear, or some new channel may be cut by which the floods escape, and the stream flows on once more, but in a different bed. A good harvest may help to set things right, however the evil has been caused, by giving some persons more means of purchasing. The outbreak of a war may cause a sudden and unexpected demand, and give a stimulus to certain trades; or some new enterprise may be devised which absorbs a good deal of the existing stocks and gives a stimulus to production. The stoppage of the process and the consequent glut comes from a deficiency of purchasing power, and when purchasing power is brought to bear, either through the enterprise of capitalists, or the necessities of Government, or the bounty of nature, the process will continue once more.

(*d*) It is in this way that the action of capitalists who take advantage of a period of depression to enlarge their premises may be a means of removing the existing evil. They purchase bricks and machinery, and this helps to set the stream in motion once more; stagnation is the evil; the least sign of a new movement indicates that the stagnation is at an end, and gives those who are possessed of money or credit more hope of being able to use it to advantage, and more willingness to try. But if the stimulus comes from a new direction, and not from the quarter in which the original obstacle occurs, industry will work on somewhat different lines from those which it previously took. Some trade may have ceased to be so profitable, say the ship-building trade, and it does not recover, but capital finds remunerative employment in electric lighting or in making bicycles, and the whole industrial process goes on as fast as before, though in rather different forms.

4. (*a*) The economic difference between a prosperous and a distressed condition of the community may be most easily ‚expressed by saying that the process of production goes on very rapidly in one, and but slowly in the other. If things are made fast they are plentiful, and they may even be used to purchase the corn which cannot be supplied at home at a faster rate. There is a great deal of work done in the year in some place, and therefore there is much that is available for human use. On the other hand, in bad times there is very little done in the same time, and therefore there is very little available for use. When trade slackens off the process becomes slow, and everyone has to adjust his habits of life to a condition when less is available for use ; it is here that the shoe begins to pinch. The sign of the evil is in the glut of goods, but the cause of the evil is in the checking or slackening of the industrial process. So far as this is a general evil in a community, it can only be cured by some change that sets free some purchasing power ; in so far as it is an evil that is special to one trade, and that arises from misjudged production, it cannot be rectified by any change that would perpetuate a slower method of production,—by ‘ making work ’ in any fashion, or maintaining hand-labour to the exclusion of machine-work. This is to create new obstacles, not to make the stream flow more rapidly, and capital, with its funds for buying materials and for hiring labour, will not turn to those directions where the stream flows slowly.

(*b*) The consideration of a period of depression may have

helped to bring out the fact that in one way or another there is an enormous amount of capital which is never replaced, and which is accordingly wasted. Not merely does it cease to be used to procure income, but it altogether ceases to be. It is no longer used as capital, and it ceases to be wealth. There is the waste of capital which is involved in injudicious loans, and is represented by bonds that are not worth the paper on which they are printed. There is the waste of capital in stock that depreciates, and there is the waste of capital that cannot be realised. Goods a man may always be able to get something for, but money sunk in plant or in buildings is much more difficult to realise. This is a most obvious source of the waste of capital ; there are so many enterprises that look well on paper, and that cannot be tried without a large initial expenditure. Such is the preliminary outlay in opening mines, which prove most disappointing, or in building railways which do not pay their working expenses. But more than this, every improvement in any process of production involves the waste of a large amount of existing capital. Old plant is superseded long before it is worn out, or new inventions do away with the need for some old line of business. The great scare about gas-shares when electric lighting was first introduced, and the manner in which canal traffic has shrunk as the railway system developed, are cases in point. In all these cases there is a frightful loss to individuals and waste of capital, though the effects on the prosperity of the community are by no means the same when capital is wholly wasted in opening a useless mine, or when its use is superseded because some better means has been discovered of doing the same work.

Partly then through bad faith or human error and miscalculation, and partly through new applications of human skill superseding old ones, there is a continual waste of capital, a waste of capital that is a terrible evil, but that cannot be altogether avoided so long as man's legitimate expectations are falsified ; it is part of the price we pay for a further advance in progress. It is not easy to see that any scheme could be devised which would get rid of these elements of waste; and herein lies the lasting importance of the new formation of capital; new capital is constantly needed to repair the waste that is always going on.

(*c*) If there has been, in any serious commercial crisis, not only a collapse of credit but a great waste of capital, the depression that follows will be likely to continue for long. The relief can only come by the introduction of some new purchasing power, but if there is little capital seeking investment no new enterprise can be floated, no foreign government can borrow, and the new impulse to industry cannot be given. Similarly, since prices are so bad and trade is so slack, it is very hard to form capital; each man has to keep his business going as best he can, but he has no opportunity of saving, and enterprise is checked because it has not the material means of trying its best.

5. It is thus by the purchase of goods, the replacement of capital, the replenishing of stock of all sorts, that a time of commercial prosperity is most clearly marked. It is not merely the symptom of prosperity, as the barometer gives an indication of fine weather, it is the thing itself. And hence there have been attempts at many times to stimulate the purchase of goods by arbitrary enactments, like the seventeenth century statutes for burying in wool. Such enactments did give greater prosperity to some one industry, and did attract capital to it; whether there was any advantage in changing the direction of the employment of capital may well be doubted; the statutes had the immediate effect that was intended, and made that industry more prosperous for the time. Similarly, when credit is inflated and prices are high, there may be times of feverish prosperity when production is going on most rapidly, all mills busy, and employers eager to hire more hands; it is real prosperity while it lasts; unfortunately experience shows that such prosperity does not last long, and that rapid production, though good in its way, is not the only thing we have to look to. Commercial prosperity is well, but there are also advantages in industrial stability.

CHAPTER X.

THE DIRECTION OF CAPITAL.

I. The Fluidity of Labour and of Capital.

1. WHENEVER the replacement of capital by purchase occurs, there generally is more or less opportunity for either continuing to use capital in the same direction as before or for applying it differently; it is comparatively easy to change the character of commercial speculations, but it may be hard to withdraw from an old industry or try a new one. If the man of enterprise has a great deal of capital invested in plant and buildings he will not be able to withdraw his capital suddenly, but he may withdraw a good deal of it gradually, if the business is not remunerative, by simply refraining from any additional outlay. Every penny that he uses for repairs, or for substituting new machinery for old, is a farther purchase of stock for his old trade; and in so far as he refrains from locking up more capital in the business he is keeping himself free to transfer his capital to some more profitable business if he can find one. The distinction between capital that is fixed in a particular trade and circulating capital cannot be easily defined for all the different kinds of industry, rural and urban, in precisely the same terms, because it depends on things, and not on what passes in the man's mind. No form of capital is absolutely permanent since all wears out in time, and the distinction turns on the frequency with which a man has to restore any part of his stock-in-trade; his tools and buildings are relatively permanent; his fund for hiring labour and his stock of material has to be constantly replenished,

and the man whose capital is chiefly in the form of circulating capital will have less difficulty in altering the direction in which he employs it than the man whose capital is chiefly fixed in tools or buildings of a permanent character. But whatever the difficulty may be in diverting capital from an employment in which it is already engaged, there is always choice as to how to use new capital when it is formed.

2. So far as capital that is free to be directly or indirectly applied to industry or commerce is concerned, the main element in determining the owner as to the direction in which he shall use his capital will be the public demand for some article. If the public demand for any object is active, prices will be high; the manufacturer will be glad to employ more capital in turning out goods as fast as possible, while new men will set up as competitors in a profitable business. On the other hand, the man of enterprise may fancy that he can stimulate public demand by supplying requirements in a better or cheaper fashion than has hitherto been done ; he hopes to use his capital so as to call forth a public demand. In either case it is the forecast of the capitalists—those who possess it, or those who have credit enough to borrow it—as to the probable demand and probable purchases made by the public, that determines the direction in which they use this wealth. If they forecast badly, and the public demand does not meet their expectations, it is so much the worse for them, and their wealth will be wasted; the fact that so much capital is wasted goes to show how often there are miscalculations about the public taste. But it remains true that the public requirements and public purchasing determines the direction in which capital is employed, even though capitalists are not always perfectly wise in interpreting the probable wishes of the public. One of the first great advantages of the co-operative societies and their association in wholesale societies is that they have the best opportunities of forecasting the tastes and requirements of the working-class public for whom they cater. It is obvious too that while rapidity in the replacement of capital is the feature of a period of commercial prosperity, facility in the change of the direction of capital is a condition

which enables the public to have what it wants on the easiest terms and at shortest notice.   If the public is fickle and always changing in its tastes and requirements, there will be a great waste of capital in the process of catering for it ; it is an extravagance to be always chopping and changing, but at the same time the possibility of doing so shows that the economic organism is highly flexible as well as highly powerful. It is ready to adapt itself to a change for the better or for the worse in public requirements.

3. The waste which is involved in changing from one direction to another is obvious when we consider the part of the capitalist's fund which is used for tools and buildings. But the mischief is more noticeable when we look at the part of capital which is employed in hiring labour.   There is a change in public requirements, and a certain trade—the Coventry ribbon-trade—declines.   Manufacturers withdraw their capital so far as they can, and do not continue to hire labour for this sort of production ; nobody knows at first whether it is a mere temporary depression or whether it is a permanent change in public requirements, except in those cases where machinery supersedes labour and there is a change, not in the public taste, but in the need of labour to supply it.   Some of those who earn their bread by the industry are thrown out of employment, and others are hired on such terms that they have to go short.   It may be most difficult for them to find any employment ; they may be highly skilled labourers with hands accustomed to fine work, who dare not break stones or pick oakum.   In the meantime no wages are coming in, the home gets more and more bare, and the man gets weaker in body and less fitted in habit for work when employment becomes open to him.   It is clear that the sooner this state of things can be brought to an end the better, and it can only be brought to an end satisfactorily in one way,—by giving the greatest possible facilities for labour to become fluid and to follow the direction which is taken by capital.   For though in times of general depression there may be no fresh call for labour from any side, the progress of enterprise is continually breaking ground in new

directions. Capitalists may see some chance of planting a new industry in the very place where the old has disappeared,—as the cocoa-nut matting manufacturè has been localised in the room of the old Sudbury weaving, or as a cotton mill and bicycle works have sprung up at Coventry. This is the most satisfactory way out of the evil, because the opportunity is opened for hiring labour in a place where unemployed labour abounds. But it is not always easy to hit on a trade which can be settled in the place of a decaying industry, and the old hands may not have the training which will enable them to learn and to work at the new craft. The technical education given in secondary schools has in all probability this one advantage over the old system of apprenticeship, that it does something to give a man this facility of adapting himself to a new employment that opens up. But when capital cannot bring a new emplpyment to the unemployed men in a town it is necessary that they should be able to migrate or emigrate to places where industry is flourishing, or at least continuing, and where there is a fair chance that they will be hired. Everything that promotes the fluidity of labour, and that renders it possible for a man to take advantage of new or of better opportunities of employment, is a vast benefit to the artisan. Labour bureaus that tell him the districts where work may be sought for do much to alleviate the distress which arises from the fluctuations of trade or the changes of trade. Great as the waste of capital may be in any change of direction, capital is much more fluid than labour, and flows more easily—with less loss and less privation—than the man who is out of employment and has to pay his travelling expenses in looking for work, and who, when he finds it, has to break up his home and move his household. These evils are at least diminished by everything that renders it more easy for labour to adapt itself to the change of public requirements, as shown by the change of the direction of capital.

4. So far as fluctuations in trade and the depression of trade are due to the failure of the capitalist to forecast the public demand, they are a social evil which it is most desir-

able to diminish; they lead to a waste of capital and terrible privation to the labourer, and the more industry is organised on a large scale under the management of one or two firms who can feel the pulse of the whole trade the less likely is this to occur. But some of the changes in the direction of industry are due to real changes in public requirements, or to new discoveries and inventions. The migration of many iron works from the Midlands to South Wales has been forced on by the desire of the owners to avoid costly railway rates. The working out of certain natural products,—coal or other minerals, or a change in the habits of fish, may affect other districts; while the progress of machinery is continually superseding domestic and hand industry and drawing the workers into factories. Progress involves change, and change in the direction of industry as well as change in other ways. While great mischief and misery accompanies every such change, true philanthropy will not endeavour to set limits to the change, but to enable the labourer to adapt himself to the inevitable possibility of change as readily as may be.

5. (*a*) From this point of view it appears that there can be no greater mischief done to the labourer than that of inducing him to cling to a doomed industry; that is, an industry which is being obviously superseded and must necessarily die out. To help a man to drag on a miserable existence as a hand-loom weaver and to encourage him to train up his children to it is not a kindness; there are parts of the country, as Ceres in Fife and Church Stretton in Shropshire, where it lingers on; and possibly through the peculiarities of local requirements it may be continued indefinitely in such places. But on the whole it is dying out; and wherever it is a struggling industry it is unlikely to revive. True philanthropy will endeavour to make the change as easy as may be, and tide over the transition with as little suffering as possible by temporary relief, if need be, but it will never tempt men to condemn themselves to a life-long and hopeless struggle by encouraging them to remain in a decaying industry.

(*b*) This matter is of considerable importance in regard to certain branches of rural employment. The widening commerce of the present day has enabled us to draw our corn from the most distant and fertile regions in the world, and has thus caused the British farmer to feel the effects of a fierce competition. This may possibly lead to considerable changes in British agriculture, and give more scope for market gardening and dairy farming, on one hand, and for pasture farming on the other. It may lead to a change in the character of British agriculture and a corresponding substitution of small holdings and large ranches for our present farms. But in so far as our present arable farming continues, it is not likely that the verdict of last century will be reversed, and that small holdings will prove superior to large, or that a cultivating peasantry will weather the storm more successfully than the capitalist farmer. But, if British agriculture is to undergo a change, it will be most likely to do so in the outlying districts and poor soils which present the greatest difficulties to the cultivators. The Skye crofter and the Galway peasant have to bear the brunt of the struggle under which many English farmers have succumbed, and they have to bear it while they still practice such modes of cultivation as proved the ruin of the English yeomanry. Politicians may be wise who desire to root these men firmly to the soil, so as to provide a population from which recruits may be drawn for the British army. But it is not the part of true Irish patriots to condemn the finest peasantry in the world to a hopeless struggle for existence in order to attain this imperial object. Philanthropists must know that if men are unconsciously condemned to desperate and hopeless poverty they have little opportunity of improving in moral and intellectual well-being. They ought to be able to show that the Galway cottier can compete successfully with the American grower before they encourage him to attach himself more firmly to an unkindly soil. So far as the fisheries or the kelp-burning have ceased to be remunerative, his resources are diminished. If the foregoing forecast is correct, it is clear that the cottier's position is nearly as hopeless as that of the hand-loom weaver, and that the case can only be met by encouraging him to change, not by tempting him to stay as he is.

II. Productive and Unproductive Consumption.

1. If there is no change in the direction of industry, the public will continue to purchase, and the capitalists will have their capital replaced. If this process goes on fast there will be a time of prosperity, and if it goes on slowly there will be a time of stagnation; but the industry of the country will continue along the same lines. But if public demand changes it may alter in one of two ways; there may be a greater demand on the part of the public for the things that are requisite for maintaining the processes of production, or there may be a greater demand for the things that are used up without helping to further production. Technically there may be an increased demand for articles of productive consumption, and there may be an increased demand for articles of unproductive consumption,—on the one hand for tools and food, on the other for flowers and perfumes. If either of these is an increased demand, and not made at the expense of some existing demand, it will undoubtedly tend towards increased commercial prosperity; it gives a new opportunity of employing capital and a new occasion of hiring labour, and in such a case the effects of all kinds of expenditure are similar.

2. But we must also look at the case where there is a change in the public demand, and the new things are sought for in preference to something that has been previously supplied. There will of course be all the evils that arise in the change from one kind of employment of capital to another, with the subsequent privation of the labourers in adapting themselves to the new conditions. If people had fewer hangings in their rooms and spent the money instead in decorating more with cut flowers, there would be less employment for the weavers of curtains than before and more employment for gardeners. It is possible in such a

case that the change would be from an industry in which labour played relatively a small part, because machines are much employed, to one where a large part of the capitalist's fund consists of means for hiring labour; such changes in the direction of industry may be immediately beneficial by calling out a demand for labour, entirely irrespective of the manner in which the commodities obtained are eventually consumed. In order to see the full significance of such a change, however, we must try to view the matter in its ulterior rather than its immediate effects, and to contrast the results of a gradual change by which more and more productive consumption is substituted for unproductive on the one hand, or unproductive consumption increased at the expense of productive on the other.

(*a*) If there is an increasing productive consumption, then more and more capital will be directed into furnishing the requirements for future production, that is to say, tools and food. It may be assumed, since Malthus published his *Essay*, that when more food is available population will increase; and thus there will be a steady tendency to provide the two great forces which carry on the work of production,—tools and food. It must be remembered, of course, that there cannot be an infinite increase in the supply of food, or an absolutely unlimited addition to the numbers of the population; but as capital and labour were set free by improvements in any other direction, they could be applied with increasing enterprise to wring more food from the soil. The continuous increase of productive consumption at the expense of unproductive would apparently lead, in so far as other social habits were unchanged, to a larger and larger mass of population on the globe engaged more and more strenuously in the production of wealth, and peopling up to the limit which each increase in production supplied.

If, however, we look at a smaller area, say at any single country, we may say that the increase of productive consumption at the expense of unproductive renders any country rich in tools and buildings and in the means of supporting labour. With these requisites the country will be able to supply its wants whatever they are, and to meet any un-expected demand upon its resources,—such as a war,—more easily than could otherwise be the case. It has a large population on which to draw for recruits, and plenty of appliances for equipping them satisfactorily.

(*b*) But the war itself is an unproductive expenditure; supposing it continues for some time, there will of course be an active demand for munitions of war, and those who supply them will enjoy great prosperity for the time which kindred trades will share. But there will be a drain of men to go to fight; they will be diverted from cultivating the ground and producing more food, and the arable area may decrease, especially if the army is victualled abroad; and the resources of the country, instead of being devoted to the replenishing of its stock of tools and appliances, will be blown away with no material result. The war may be positively necessary, but for all that it is costly, because it diverts the energy of the nation into supplying means of unproductive consumption, and thus leaves it less well supplied with a stock of buildings and tools, and less well able to provide a proper supply of food. Whether the expense of the war is met by heavy taxes, or by borrowing and thus spread over a period of years, is unimportant from this point of view. All that has to be noticed is that the expenditure, however wise and how-ever necessary, is unproductive, and that the country is exhausted by such expenditure, and less able to continue the production of wealth at the old rate and in the old way when peace returns. The decay of a territory like the Southern States, where the struggle was waged with such severity, and where, when it was over, there was difficulty in borrowing capital to start industry afresh, may serve to illustrate the nature of the enormous evil that is caused by unproductive consumption.

(*c*) Comparing the two, then, it appears that an increase of productive at the expense of unproductive consumption in any nation tends to increase the facilities which it enjoys for continuing to carry on the industrial processes as rapidly or with increasing rapidity; while the substitution of unproductive for productive consumption tends to material exhaustion and to a state where it can only carry on industrial processes with difficulty and slowly. A change in public requirements which turns capital from one direction to another and to making articles of luxury instead of requisites of production, tends towards national impoverishment; unless indeed the articles of luxury are produced for export and for foreign consumption; in such case this kind of industry may be the easiest means by which a community can buy, and therefore provide itself with certain requisites of future production it cannot produce. The Scilly islanders may do well to grow flowers in order to purchase corn and clothes and spades.

3. But it is obvious that in every country there is likely to be a certain amount of both kinds of production, and that the tendency to exhaustion only arises when unproductive is substituted for productive consumption, or, as we may say, trenches upon it. We might also measure the wealth of any community by noticing the amount of riches it can devote to unproductive consumption without trenching on the supply of the requisites of production. If the inhabitants of any land are able to live in great luxury for a long period without exhausting the resources of their country and its dependencies, and without trenching on the requisites of future production, it must be a very wealthy land. There was such exhaustion in ancient Rome, for the wealthy citizens not only drained the resources of Italy, but impoverished the provinces so that they could offer no effective resistance to the barbarians.

(*a*) The possibility of unproductive consumption without exhaustion is the great indication of a wealthy nation. It would seem to follow that, since it is good to be wealthy, it is good also to have a large unproductive expenditure. And this is so. It is not the chief end of man to produce more goods, or to provide the requisites of production in greater and greater abundance. It is a good thing to have plenty to spend, so long as you spend it well. The question of productive and unproductive consumption is important, for in it lies the secret of the continuance of national prosperity; but it is not so important as the question whether the unproductive consumption of the nation is wise or unwise, for therein lies the secret of the improvement or the degradation of the national life.

(*b*) Expenditure on education and art and the cultivation of taste and the improvement of human faculty is unproductive; only in slave countries can the training of human beings be regarded as the production of marketable wares. The man who teaches may be a useful person; and even if he is not he may deserve to be paid for doing his best to improve human faculties and store human minds. All the expenditure that is made in investigation, and on moral or religious culture, is unproductive; it is not therefore unwise, for indeed it is the possibility of securing such things in fuller measure that makes wealth worth having at all.

But the unproductive consumption that merely gratifies passing whims, that ministers to selfishness on the one hand and rouses bitterness and jealousy on the other, this is indeed an evil; not because it does not tend to the production of more wealth, but because it is a misuse of existing wealth that breeds personal sin and social disorder.

Wealth is not to be pursued for its own sake but in order that it may be well and wisely used. The wealth that is not used for the production of more wealth is not necessarily wasted; it may be applied to much better purpose, as it may be used for much worse. And here it would seem that the consideration of the practical matters connected with capital can take us no further, for we are brought face to face with an ethical question as to the right and the wrong use of wealth when we have got it.

PART III

PERSONAL DUTY.

——•■•——

CHAPTER XI.

PERSONAL RESPONSIBILITY.

IT is a matter of common complaint in the present day against Political Economy that it is either immoral or non-moral. To the hasty reader it has seemed to advocate selfishness, and there has been some excuse for this accusation. In recent times, however, economists have endeavoured to evade it by assuming an attitude of rigorous and scientific impartiality. They do not profess to tell us what ought to happen but only what tends to happen under certain assumed circumstances—in a regime of free competition; if they lay stress on self-interest, it is because self-interest is so dominant in human nature as we know it. But after all there are some of us who are eager not only to understand what tends to happen in society as it is, but also to see how far it is possible to hope that society may be kept from falling to a lower level in matters of right and wrong, and how individuals may be encouraged to struggle to live by a better standard than that which is current, and which economic science assumes as normal.

Nor in so doing are we called upon to break fresh ground.

Questions of duty in various economic relations were discussed with much acuteness for centuries before the laws of supply and demand were formulated. The cases these earlier students had to consider were very different from those which occur in the present day, but it may serve as a suitable introduction to the problems we have to face in our complicated society if we try to understand the principles on which the schoolmen decided the simpler questions which they were called on to consider.

Those who have interested themselves in trying to trace the history of economic doctrine in Christendom, find familiar topics treated from a standpoint that differs curiously from our own, when they turn to mediaeval writers like Aquinas. Economic affairs are discussed not with the view of practically promoting prosperity of the country as the mercantilists tried; nor, as modern economists do, with the view of stating in general terms the principles on which people do habitually act; but rather with the intention of discriminating right from wrong in personal conduct. These students might perhaps have admitted that, as modern economists assume, a man in driving his business tried to secure as much gain as he could for himself,—that this tended to happen; and they knew that this was to some extent natural, and that it was right for a man to do with his might whatever his hands found to do. Yet they also knew that in all these things there was a danger of falling into sin. They wished to discuss how to draw a line which should show where men were falling into wrong in their monetary transactions,—for what actions they were to be condemned, and, if they persisted in them, excommunicated. They thus came to set themselves to define what was wrong. It was not their business to lay down a hard and fast scheme of duty in regard to industry; they found the scheme of secular duty for their day was fairly expounded by the example of the monasteries—with a personal discipline of poverty, chastity, and obedience, a corporate care for the dependents on their estates, and a readiness to devote the gains of their trade to the glory of God in the beautiful fanes they raised for His worship.   The cultivation of Christian graces in secular affairs, charity and so forth, were not the subject-matter they had primarily in hand in writing about economics; but they wanted to denounce what was wicked, and to show when men were to be blamed for the manner in which they did their business.

I. Degrees of Responsibility.

1. These questions of wrong-doing and blame were much simpler in mediaeval times than they are now; partly because transactions of every kind were less complex, but chiefly because in any case of wrong-doing it was much easier to say who was to blame, while we must take account of different degrees of responsibility.   If work was badly done, the fault could be brought home to a bad workman, and it could be seen that he had been careless.   But now that goods are manufactured in distant places, or vamped up in quantities to suit a public demand for cheap and inferior articles, it is very hard to say that the fault lies with any one in particular.   No man is to be condemned for what he cannot help and does on external compulsion; a hero may resist the compulsion and perish, but a man is not necessarily guilty because he has failed to show himself a hero. In industry and trade as they were carried on in mediaeval times it was generally possible to bring home to any fraudulent or extortionate dealer that he was the guilty person; whereas in our complicated social system to-day it is very hard to say how far any man is free from external pressure and therefore is personally to blame.

At the same time we may see that the difficulty of assigning the direct responsibility for any mischief does not exonerate us from the duty of trying to detect where the mischief lies; it only makes it necessary for us to examine the matter more closely than the schoolmen were forced to do.   If wrong occurs, not through personal greed, but because the habits of society or the law of the land is unsatisfactory, then every member of society and every free citizen is *indirectly responsible* for the mischief. We shall have to ask how far is any wrong due to personal sin, and therefore to be corrected by rousing the sense of personal duty, or by meting out personal punishment? or how far is it due to social conventions and customs and laws for which all citizens are indirectly responsible? Hence we may say that personal responsibility is not less real than in old times. We are just as much bound to discharge that responsibility, but it has to be discharged in two distinct ways : not only in the affairs that practically are under our own present control and where the responsibility is direct and complete, but in affairs that can only be controlled and remedied by altering the customs of society and the law of the land; then we are responsible in a less degree, because indirectly, but our responsibility is none the less real. This indirect responsibility could formerly be dealt with as the duty of the Prince ; he was responsible for the good government and the well-being of the people committed to his charge, but it has now come to be the indirect responsibility of each free citizen, as it was not in the times of feudal monarchies.

2. There are many cases where the degree of responsibility has to be considered before we attempt to fix the degree of blame. Some years ago a considerable excitement was caused by the testimony of a working shipwright at Liverpool who explained the character of the very insufficient repairs he had been ordered to make in a ship, which was sent out in an utterly unseaworthy condition. It was said he ought not to have done such insufficient work under any circumstances, but the dishonesty was not on his part ; he earned what he was paid to do, and he was not responsible for it, though he was the agent by whom it was done. He did his own task ; the evil was that he was set to do the wrong kind of work, and to repair badly. But if he had played the heroic part, he would have been thrown on the world, and the fraudulent repairs would have been executed by someone else; his heroism would not have prevented the mischief being done. It seems to me he was not to be blamed for doing the bad work under protest ; for this he was not directly responsible, he was

acting under orders. He was also right in discharging his indirect responsibility, and calling attention to the evil at which others had connived, in the hope that it might be remedied by such legislation as Mr. Plimsoll proposed.

Again, at the time of the first Factory Acts there were employers who felt that the women and children were being seriously injured by the drudgery to which they were exposed, and that their hours ought to be shorter. They were, however, engaged in a business where the competition was keen, and where they may have honestly believed they could not alter the conditions of work without incurring certain ruin. It might have been heroic to court ruin, but it would not really have benefited the employers in that mill, and it might have put obstacles in the way of a more general movement. It may at least be argued that they were right to carry on their business personally on the lines of which they did not approve, and to endeavour to exercise their influence indirectly, by urging that a restrictive law should be passed for the whole country.

3. There is thus a distinct difference between any mischief for which we are personally responsible, and any mischief that arises out of our conduct, but for which we are not personally to blame because of external pressure. There is a much more strict obligation in regard to duties that fall within our own personal power than in regard to matters for which we have, in common with many others, only an indirect responsibility; what is everybody's business is too often nobody's business. We cannot rate too highly the importance of the work done by those who make public business their own business, and thus prove themselves to be really good citizens.

On the whole, however, current opinion is inclined to ignore degrees of responsibility and is satisfied with denouncing the agents through whom any hardship is wrought, without considering sufficiently where the ultimate responsibility lies. There are plenty of people who go looking for bargains, and purchase their furniture or their clothes at prices that ought at least to suggest that there is something

wrong somewhere about the means employed for producing such goods. It is all very well to denounce
sweaters, but those who do so ought to be perfectly clear
that their own hands are clean, and that their preference for
cheap goods does not encourage dealers to cater for this
requirement, so that they themselves are ultimately, though
indirectly, responsible for some of the evil they deplore.
There is always this double responsibility to be looked to,
responsibility for not doing our best to cure the evil, and
responsibility for its existence. In the present state of
society and in regard to the great mischiefs of the present
day—overcrowding, starvation wages, and so forth—it is
rarely that any individual can be definitely singled out for
blame. It is the divided responsibility, or the indirect responsibility, of many unthinking persons that makes the
whole so difficult to deal with. But in the simpler society of
mediaeval times there was no such divided responsibility;
the King, and not the people, was responsible for bad laws,
and this or that man could be definitely pointed out as
blameable for bad goods or unfair gain.

There are very considerable difficulties about fulfilling this
indirect responsibility for the good condition of the country
in the obvious way, by using the influence each citizen
possesses in favour of governmental interference to prevent
wrong. But it may at least simplify the matter if we can see
a clear rule as to cases where government interference is
distinctly advisable.

(*a*) The life and effective vigour of the population is one of
the most precious of material resources ; and if any business
is so conducted as to be seriously injuring them, then there
can be no doubt that it is well to prohibit the continuance of
practices of the kind. Thus, if little children are worked for
long hours, and must necessarily, if they survive at all, be
miserable and weakly men and women, it is obviously wise
to interfere to prevent their working for such long hours.
Legislation which aims at removing a positive evil, the
economic effects of which are palpable, has very strong evidence in its favour. It is difficult to conceive any reasons

for accepting such a state of affairs as inevitable, and for refusing to try to alter it by any method that is available. But the case is altered somewhat if the object is, not to redress an obvious evil, but to provide better opportunities for any class. Here we are at once brought face to face with a speculation as to how the opportunities will be used. Some men may make one forecast, and some another. It may be that the reduction of manual labour to eight hours would give the opportunity of a better life to many artisans, the opportunity of better work during working hours, and of larger human interest in times of leisure. There is, after all, an element of uncertainty; it is not quite clear that the shorter hours will be spent in more diligent and careful work; it is not clear that the hours of leisure will be wisely used, and it is possible that there may be serious loss in consequence of the change both to employers and employed. Are we wise to run the risk? In such a question of practical politics as this the whole decision must turn on the estimate we make of certain probabilities. According to temperament, some men will make a more favourable and some a less favourable forecast; and the whole is removed from the sphere of rational argument into speculating on probabilities. There can be no such plain duty to give better opportunities—the value of which depends on the way in which they are used—as there is to put down positive mischief.

(*b*) On the other hand, in so far as it seems desirable to interfere, with the view of giving better opportunities, there is on the whole less likelihood of misuse, when they are given in connexion with work. Thus, the eight hours' day would be a boon to the man who worked, but it would make no difference to the man who did not work at all. On the other hand, the distributions of corn among the Romans, and the public provision for their amusement, were demoralising. The custom gave them a good time, but it did not really fit them to be more useful members of society. It is, of course, good that people should be amused—it is a wholesome thing; if the monotony of life is relieved they will be brighter and more cheerful. But how far is it right that they should be amused at the public expense, i. e. that one set of people should be taxed to provide amusement for others? It is certainly doubtful. All that private munificence does for public recreation is good, but how far is it a duty to provide for recreation out of public funds? How far is it demoralising? All this has to be weighed carefully with special reference to the precise form of each particular proposal, and there can be no such plain duty to provide facilities for recreation as there is to prohibit positive evils.

(*c*) It may appear that this is merely a verbal distinction, and that every improvement in the condition of life might be expressed in either fashion. They provide better opportunities just because they redress evils. Perhaps the distinction may be marked most clearly by appealing to a physical standard. Where the death-rate rises, or where there are new diseases, or where measurements show that the population is deteriorating, there is positive evil, and we are bound to seek for the causes and try to remedy them; but where no such evidence can be adduced a reform may be much needed, but there is not the same plain call for governmental inquiry and intervention.

This distinction, in so far as it can be clearly drawn, illustrates the old adage that it is impossible to make men moral by act of Parliament. All that legislation can do is to give men better opportunities of making themselves moral. It may remove crying evils, but it cannot do positive good; it can only provide the opportunity for good. If these new opportunities are to serve any useful purpose there must be some power of using them aright; there must be higher ideals of how to spend time and money, and force of will to give them effect. It is too often assumed that all we have to consider with the view of improving mankind is the possibility of changing their circumstances; but the real difficulty lies in changing them so that they shall take advantage of improved circumstances. The attractive force of personal kindness and personal sympathy must not be left out of account in this connexion, and private charity may call forth new vigour where relief at the public expense would only degrade. It appears that public duty calls on us to prevent retrogression, but that it is private benevolence and personal sympathy that does most to elevate.

4. It is comparatively easy to take a part and use influence in favour of some legislative measure when attention is once directed to a crying evil; the constitution of the country marks out the manner in which each man may exercise his duty as a good citizen. It is far harder to know how to act in regard to the other indirect responsibility which falls on all those who consume goods which are produced by sweating. The ordinary purchaser is quite incapable of judging accurately of the quality of the goods he buys, and has not the means of informing himself as to the conditions of production. He may feel that the rage for cheapness induces traders to cut things as fine as may be; but if he pays a high price he will himself be poorer, and how can he tell who will be better off? The single individual is so little informed, and so little able to procure information, that he can hardly be held to be bound to enquire for himself; though he may feel it a duty to discontinue dealing with any firm who are known to be guilty of oppressive conduct, and he may also be expected to inform himself carefully before he changes his custom from respectable traders who have served him well, on the mere grounds that somebody else will supply goods, called by the same names, for less money. But the range of personal influence exerted in such fashion is infinitesimal; the mischief is to a great extent due to the system of letting work on contract, and though this may be a convenient method for guarding against fraud, it neither conduces to the supply of good work nor to favourable conditions for the producer. If large firms or public departments could so far count on honest service as to be able to check the work done for them accurately, and to dispense with the convenient method of letting contracts, the pressure which has given rise to sweating would be very greatly reduced.

II.   Scholastic Distinctions in regard to the Forms of Bargains.

1. This, then, is one broad distinction between the problems about economic duty in mediaeval and in modern times. The schoolmen dealt chiefly with direct responsibility, while we have to deal with different degrees of responsibility; and we find it specially hard to fulfil our indirect responsibilities. It is almost to restate the same thing in other terms when we say they could concentrate their attention on the bargains between one man and another, without following out the indirect bearings of the transactions very far. Society was less complex, and it was possible for men to isolate separate bargains and examine the *forms* under which they were contracted, and then to pronounce them to be fair or unfair. Their idea of fair gain apparently was that it accrued because of real work done; that a service was rendered, and the man was remunerated for what he did; but that gain was unfair when it was secured without any corresponding service, when it was obtained not by doing something for someone, but at somebody's expense.

(*a*) For example, the merchant who brought wine to this country might fairly be remunerated for his trouble in doing so, and when it was sold in the interior of the country there was an allowance for the cost of carriage. The Cambridge dons were constantly inclined to complain that they were charged more for their wine than the Oxford dons; but the excellence of the water-way from the great mart at London doubtless favoured the University situated in the Thames Valley, even though Cambridge had easy communication with Lynn. The gain which the trader made in this fashion was a legitimate return for the trouble he took in supplying the English consumers in their own towns with a foreign commodity; they recognised the point which modern economists insist on, when they class those who are engaged in the carrying trades among productive labourers. But if the traders monopolised the whole supply of wine and sold it at a dearer rate, with a profit that covered a great deal more than remuneration for their trouble, then they were getting a gain at the expense of the consumer, and this was held to be unfair; the whole of the legislation against forestallers and engrossers rested on this principle. They tried to buy up goods so that they might rule the market, and make a profit at the expense of consumers, without any adequate exertion or service which they themselves rendered. To gain by 'making a corner,' or by creating an artificial scarcity, was to be guilty of extorting from another; this extortion, whether practised by the wealthy against the poor, or by the labourers against their employers, was condemned alike in all cases. To take advantage of a man's need, or to aggravate a man's need for the sake of getting more gain, was conduct which they denounced in all its forms.

(*b*) The moralists and legislators of the middle ages accordingly set themselves to prohibit transactions which gave the opportunity for extortion, where it might lurk without any one being able to check it and see for certain that he was being fairly treated. The operations of middlemen would often open larger markets and tend towards the benefit of producers and consumers alike, while the operations of engrossers, like corn-factors, tended to equalise prices over any period. They did not work altogether for evil, and as time went on, and the social benefits they conferred became more obvious, free scope was given for their operations. But dealings of this sort, though indirectly beneficial, did give opportunities for unscrupulous men to make a profit at the expense of the producer or the consumer, and hence for many generations transactions of this sort were forbidden.

In regard to monetary affairs there was a special difficulty in forming any estimate as to the fair equivalent which a man with a fund of money might obtain for the services he rendered, in whatever way he used it. He was hedged in on every side. If he attempted to carry on business as an exchanger, for profit, he was apt to infringe the privileges of the crown and the mint. If he sought to lend money to neighbours who needed it, and asked for interest on the money, he found he was under the suspicion of trading on their necessities. In all these various cases there was special opportunity for taking advantage of men's ignorance or of their need; there was the greatest danger that extortion would be practised, and therefore mediaeval legislation, both ecclesiastical and civil, discouraged or prohibited any one from making his living in such ways. But the restrictions in regard to commerce were far less frequent than those for other employments of money. On the whole it was possible for the moneyed man to enter into partnership with others and share the risks and the profits of a venture; even here such restrictions might be forced on him, in the interest of the consumer, as to destroy all possibility of gain; but this field of enterprise was open to all who would take the risks. It was only when a man tried to bargain himself out of risks, and at the same time endeavoured to secure a gain for certain, that they felt he was driving a one-sided and unfair bargain. He was trying to secure himself against possible loss, which was fair enough; but he was also trying to secure a gain for himself, however the venture turned out, and this gave rise to the danger of extortion.

The lender, according to mediaeval notions, was perfectly justified in trying to secure himself against loss of the principal by taking a pledge for the return of his money. But if he chose to secure himself against loss in the course of trade, he had no fair claim to remuneration as well. Apparently the schoolmen considered that the essence of the service which the moneyed man rendered lay in his undertaking the risks of business, and that if he bargained himself out of the risks he had no claim to any gain from business. He might make his choice, and have his principal secured to him and get no gain, or he might risk his principal and reap a contingent gain; but he appeared to be dealing very hardly if he insisted on both demands,—on securing himself against possible loss, and bargaining for a definite and certain gain. The man who lent his money on security without asking for interest was doing a charitable thing,—it was a thoroughly Christian act. The man who went into partnership in business and risked his money in the hope of a contingent gain, deserved the gain that accrued; but the man who secured himself and demanded gain as well was making a bargain by which he might gain at another's expense, and he was falling into sin.

(*c*) They would not have denied that the lender did the man who borrowed a real service; they recognised that it was a real charity to assist him in this way. The man who throws a rope to a drowning man does him a real service, but we should condemn the conduct of any one who tried to bargain with the drowning man before throwing him the rope, and charged, not an equivalent for his own trouble in rendering the service, but as much as the man could be got to pay rather than lose his life. The schoolmen saw no means of assessing in terms of money an equivalent for the service the moneyed man renders, when he bargains himself out of all risks; they could frame no standard of what was fair, and they knew that, as a matter of fact, moneyed men were only too apt to take advantage of the needs of others so as to make large gains for themselves. As has been pointed out above, there was little scope for the employment of money in ordinary business in mediaeval times. Those who borrowed did not do so in order to trade, for they could hardly have made much profit for themselves with money on which they paid 40 per cent. They borrowed because there was some special pressure, like unexpected demand for royal or papal taxation, or because they wished to undertake some great work at once, or fit out a military expedition. They usually borrowed, because they had occasion for ready money in order to meet some expense, and therefore they were more or less in the power of the lender; the pressure which forced them to borrow at all, would also force them to agree to extortionate terms. In this way a man who was really wealthy might, through a temporary need for ready money, get drawn into a ruinous agreement by which his whole property should be gradually drained. The temporary need might be converted into a permanent and intolerable burden if the lender máde an unscrupulous use of his opportunity for extortion.

The mere *form* of the agreement appeared to the schoolmen to indicate sufficiently whether there was room for extortion or not. They did not feel it necessary to take account of the *rate* of gain for which the lender bargained; for they held that if he was secured against loss he had all the consideration he could fairly demand, and that any extra gain only represented the need of the borrower, not an equivalent of the service rendered by the lender. A man had a right to require that his own should be restored to him and to take security; he had a right to require that it should be returned at a given date; but in the circumstances of the day, and with the very limited field for investment which was then available, it seemed impossible to assign any rational grounds for demanding more than this; and therefore it seemed impossible that a lender could justify such a demand. That the borrower was willing to pay was perfectly true; but that did not make it right for the lender to take advantage of his desire to escape from a present evil at the expense of involving himself with future liabilities. Any bargain which, while securing the principal, also demanded interest, appeared from its very form to be extortionate, since it seemed to show that the moneyed man was taking advantage of the borrower's need.

2. In the sixteenth century, however, it began to be generally felt among business men, as had not been the case in preceding centuries, that the old distinction which rested on the form of the bargain was unsatisfactory. There were many cases in which loans, though usurious in form, were not extortionate as a matter of fact. If a merchant made on an average 10 per cent. by the use of capital, he could easily afford to borrow at 6 per cent.; the man who bargained to receive 6 per cent. from a merchant who gained more largely still by the use he made of the capital borrowed, could not be regarded as guilty of extortion. During the sixteenth century there was an extraordinary stimulus given to English industry and commerce, and many men were eager to borrow, not for the sake of relieving themselves from difficulties, but to enlarge their trade, or to commence trading. This was a state of society which the schoolmen had not contemplated; and the modern conscience felt that there was no harm in

many bargains made in forms which they had condemned. The Tudors and Stuarts attempted to draw a new kind of distinction between extortionate and fair monetary transactions by limiting the rate of interest. They passed permissive bills which allowed men to bargain for definite gain on secured loans, so long as the gain was limited to a comparatively low rate; but this sort of regulation was indefensible in principle and could not be enforced in practice,—though it survived till Jeremy Bentham dealt it a death-blow.

The logic of facts has thus condemned these attempts to distinguish between what is extortionate and what is fair in regard to lending. The scholastic distinction, according to the form of the bargains, prohibited much that was obviously harmless: if it had been maintained it would have seriously interfered with the expansion of our commerce and the development of our West Indian colonies. The Tudor rule, as gradually modified, was not susceptible of rational justification, and was evaded in practice; it was not merely useless but often injurious, and served to aggravate the evil it was designed to prevent. But even if it be impossible to draw a distinction, which can be embodied in statute law, and to draft a rule which can be enforced under penalties, it may be possible to discuss the matter so as to give counsel for personal conduct. If it were possible to frame some maxims for personal guidance in the new circumstances of the day we should at least have advanced a step; a very little step, but still a real one. There are many men who feel that the strong condemnation of usury, not only in Scripture, but among ancient moralists of all sorts, must mean something. When the secret practices of money-lenders are exposed they realise that the evil is not entirely a thing of the past, and they are anxious to see that they themselves are free from blame in this matter.

Nor is it possible to get satisfactory guidance from public opinion. Public opinion is not inclined to condemn any transaction that is concluded openly and in the light of day; but posterity may see in this, as we do in the stories of Roman spectacles, a proof that society was corrupt, not that the thing itself was right. Public opinion is apt to tend to a lower level of morality, to accept as legitimate all that the law refuses to condemn as criminal. Public opinion can only be raised by those who set a higher standard for themselves personally; they may in time impress the world with the fact that theirs is a good standard, and the law may secure the advance by condemning conduct that defies this higher standard. But it is by personal effort to attain a higher standard of virtue than that which is current, and only so, that the tone of society itself can be raised.

The pages that follow contain some suggestions as to maxims for personal guidance; these can, of course, only be put forward tentatively, and as suggestions. The distinctions which the schoolmen drew are no longer applicable, but the evil which they tried to avoid is not extinct. We can no longer be content, as they were, with looking merely at the form of the bargain; they condemned much which our consciences feel to be allowable; it cannot be wicked to take a money reward for doing what it is virtuous to do gratuitously; so long as we are sure that the money reward is reasonable and not excessive. How shall we guard ourselves against the possibility of being extortionate? They would have eschewed all bargains that might become extortionate; can we draw the line in any other way? In their day, extortion was commonly practised when the form of the bargain gave the opportunity; in our times it is perhaps exceptional. Can we find maxims which will enable us to avoid these exceptional cases of the extortion which seemed to them to be inevitably connected with lending money on security, and for a definite rate of return?

There are three different questions of duty which demand consideration; we may enquire first of all, about right and wrong as it concerns the manner in which capital is employed; secondly, right and wrong as to the rate of return received from capital; and thirdly, right and wrong as to the expenditure of income and enjoyment of wealth.

CHAPTER XII.

Duty in regard to employing Capital.

There are some kinds of business in which no one need have any scruple in engaging; there is no sort of productive employment which adapts the gifts of nature to the use of man that is a wrong way to use one's time and money. It is a duty to do such business heartily and earnestly, and to give one's mind to carrying it on as well as possible. The ethical questions in regard to such an employment must all be about the manner in which it is carried on; whether in developing the business, or in arranging its details, there are any minor dishonesties or extortions. But there may be other modes of using money which are wrong in themselves, not because of faults in the way of conducting them, but because the business itself is immoral. Thus it is illegal to keep a gambling hell; it may be profitable to do so, but it is pandering to a violent passion, and the employment is immoral, even if it is conducted with the most scrupulous regard to honesty as between the managers and those who frequent it. In the same way it is immoral to make money by dealing in slaves; this is apparently a very risky business, and the profits on successful transactions are high; but the misery it causes, especially in the kidnapping of slaves, is overwhelming, and it is wrong to do it at all, and of course wrong to make money by doing it. There are some employments, then, that are plainly immoral, while there are others that are plainly allowable. In regard to the latter we have only to consider whether we are doing a thing that is not wrong in the right way; but in presence of the existence of gambling hells, and of slave marts, we are forced to ask how we are to discriminate the allowable uses of capital from those that are to be condemned as wrong.

I. By what standard shall we discriminate?

1. There is indeed some difficulty in seeing by what standard we are to judge. There is of course a standard given by the law of the land, which treats some employments as criminal, or regards others as outside the pale of the law, so that there can be no recovery for debts. Public opinion may have a slightly higher standard; it refuses to pay much respect to a man who only just manages to evade the law, and is guilty of sharp practice; but, after all, the public memory is short, and if the sharp practice is successful, much will be condoned to the man who has risen to a position of affluence, and a little generosity will silence unfriendly criticism. But the standard on which the law acts is necessarily a low one. It can only condemn what is plainly wrong and what is proved to be wrong; it cannot take account of many forms of wrong-doing, because it is impossible to obtain evidence without opening the way for grosser mischiefs. It cannot blame a man for the indirect and distant effects of action which was in itself legitimate. It cannot adequately weigh motives and discriminate what is well-intentioned from what is malicious. And so long as this is the case we may feel that the standard it sets serves to stigmatise what is wrong, but does not hold up an ideal of what is right. We are bound to see that we do not fall below the standard set by the law of the land; but we are not necessarily right if we keep up to it. Those who from any motive allow themselves to infringe it are greatly to blame; they are, at all events, involved in the appearance of evil, and are setting a bad example; but it at best only marks out what is allowable from what is wrong, it does not lay down clearly what is right for me in my circumstances.

2. Hence we may see from another point of view the

importance of cherishing an ideal for human society; it keeps before us the goal towards which we are to move, the aim which we are to keep in view. It is an inspiring thing to have a high ideal, it is a duty to cherish it, and never to be satisfied with meaner conceptions of life; it is right to endeavour to realise it. Here we may see the influence which religion can exercise on economic action and social life. It sets before us a nobler ideal, it gives us strength to try and realise it, and to maintain it through disappointment and discouragement. Such an ideal is a personal power, inspiring personal effort; but as it takes hold of one man after another, as it is less and less imperfectly realised by one and another, it raises the tone of society. In so far as action is in accord with the ideal it may be said to be virtuous; and we ought to aim, not merely at escaping the clutches of the law by avoiding what is wrong, but at leading a virtuous life.

We may thus find a great difference of standard in regard to almost every action of ordinary life. The law stigmatises what is wrong, and leaves us to gather what is allowable; but the good man will not be satisfied with this standard; he has a higher ideal, and his conscience will not allow him to ignore or forget it. He will try to do, not only what is allowable because it is not wrong, but what is consonant with his ideal and therefore right. His conscience takes a stricter view than the law of the land, because it has the means of taking account of motive and intention as well as of word and deed. And there may therefore be frequent cases where his conscience condemns, as not right for him, what the law of the land and public opinion regard as allowable conduct. And in such a case the man who goes against his conscience and accepts the lower standard is certainly wrong, even though society may find no fault with him.

At the same time the decision of his conscience is a personal one; the action is wrong for him, with his ideal, and his knowledge of the circumstances of the case. He is called upon to guide his own conduct by his own sense of duty, but he is not justified in applying it directly to anyone else. In judging of others, we have no reason to apply a different standard from that which is current, and which is embodied in the law of the land, as set by public opinion ; we are only justified in condemning them when they fall below this standard and are guilty of doing something it stigmatises as wrong. Herein lies the importance of the principle which is so widely accepted at present, that business of every kind should be above-board, and should bear the light of day. So far as transactions are public, they will not fall below the commonly recognised standard of what is allowable ; and this is a good thing. But if no one tries to rise above the standard, and thus helps to raise it, there is a real danger that it will be gradually lowered. We cannot condemn what is done publicly and above-board by others, but we would do well to have a stricter conception of duty to apply to ourselves.

But how, it may be asked, are we to bring our ideal to bear on actual life? We may cherish an ideal of human society where there shall be no poverty and no oppression, where all shall be comfortable and none shall be surfeited with luxuries ; but such an ideal is social. It can only be realised in and by the community, and one human being cannot make a little millenium all by himself in entire disregard of his surroundings? What is the good of an ideal which seems to be a mere dream? If I cannot realise it by myself it cannot serve as a guide to my conduct.

3. Here again we come on another instance of the distinction which has been insisted on so often. We may frame our ideal for man in terms of his surroundings, or we may frame it in terms that concern him. (*a*) To picture the possible surroundings which men might have is simply to let the imagination run riot. It is idle if we call in the help of inventions and discoveries which have not yet been made ; it is merely tantalising if we content ourselves with picturing an immense improvement in human surroundings which might be made with our present powers. Every peasant with a fowl in the pot was the French King's ideal,

and it was one which an absolute monarch could have realised for a time, perhaps for a day, but he could not guarantee its continuance. This is the defect of all ideals which are framed in terms of human surroundings; we need to secure the diligence and self-restraint of the men, in order that these ideal surroundings, when once achieved, may be maintained. And hence it is simplest and wisest to frame our ideals in terms of personal motive and character; for we may be sure that if the ideal of internal and personal life were once generally realised, the externals would soon be satisfactory too. 'Life develops from within;' and a world that was peopled by unselfish and diligent men would leave but little ground for complaint so far as the material comforts of the population were concerned.

(*b*) It may be true that ideal circumstances would give the best opportunity for training ideal men, but so long as opportunities are neglected and misused the ideal circumstances would not ensure ideal men. It is best worth while to fix our attention on personal character, and to frame our ideal in terms of character, since in so far as that is attained, and the springs of human action are affected, the results of human action in the shaping of human environment will follow directly.

Such a personal ideal, too, as it takes account of motives and intentions, may afford immediate assistance in ordinary life. We cannot make everybody comfortable, but we can endeavour to see that our motives are unselfish, and we can set ourselves to be diligent in our business. In this way each single act, in this imperfect world, may be tested by our ideal. We may be able to see that conduct that is allowable according to the standard of public opinion is wrong for us, because it is inconsistent with our ideal, inasmuch as it is a selfish endeavour to gain at the expense of others, or a piece of lazy self-indulgence. An ideal expressed in terms of man's surroundings is a mere dream, for there is no security that it could be maintained even if it were introduced, and it gives us no help in regard to the means that must be taken for introducing it; but an ideal expressed in terms of personal characteristics is the greatest assistance to progress it gives us guidance at every moment of doubt, and thus prepares the way step by step for a more complete realisation.

4. It is worth while to observe, too, that those who cherish an ideal of comfortable circumstances, of easy competence and comfort for all, are inclined to look for its realisation, not to their own action, but to the doings of others. ' My modest five hundred a year will do little to diffuse general comfort, but my neighbour's five hundred a day might do much.' Hence the natural attitude to take is that of criticising the conduct of others instead of looking carefully to our own doings. It is much easier to inveigh against the greed of millionaires than it is to use £500 a year in the right way. But if our ideal is framed in terms of personal motive we shall begin by seeing that our own motives are right, and we shall be disinclined to waste our time in criticising the conduct of those who are in other circumstances than ours, and of whose motives and shortcomings we cannot judge.

It is not wicked to be rich, but it is wicked either for a rich man or a poor one to be greedy and selfish. Our morality is least likely to be confused if the ideal by which we correct the vague permissions of public opinion turns our attention to our own personal motives, which we know, rather than to those of others, about which we can only speculate.

II. The mis-employment of Capital.

Such are the available means for judging of right and wrong in economic affairs; we may now turn to view questions connected with the employment of capital in the light they afford. In doing so we shall have to distinguish the two modes of employing capital which have been discussed above, for there are at any rate different degrees of responsibility according (1) as we lend capital to other people who misuse it, or (2) misuse it ourselves by engaging in a kind of business which our consciences do not approve.

1. (*a*) The preliminary objection that such loans are in themselves wrong may perhaps be waived. This was undoubtedly the opinion of the fathers and schoolmen; but it is also clear that circumstances alter cases, and it would be

difficult to contend that such loans are always wrong at the present time. A modern official utterance of the Church of Rome did not make this bold and uncompromising assertion, and it does not seem possible to cut the Gordian knot and solve all the perplexities in a rough and ready fashion. The danger of extortion in connexion with loans, which was the practical reason for the scholastic prohibition, can be conveniently dealt with when we are considering right and wrong in regard to gain from capital, that is to say, the terms on which loans are made.

(*b*) We may then look at the case of loans to a foreign Government. According to the ordinary standard which is set by public opinion, a man lends his money in the open market, and gets his bond. The whole transaction is aboveboard, and is perfectly straightforward and simple.

But the scrupulous man may not be so easily satisfied; he may feel that he is indirectly responsible for what the Government do with his money, because he has supplied them with the means of carrying out their purpose, whatever it is. It is conceivable that the city of Geneva should desire to attract wealthy folks from all nations by establishing gaming-saloons, and that it would endeavour to float a loan so as to carry out this scheme in the most magnificent fashion. Those who knew the object to which the loan was to be applied, and who lent their capital to enable the city to start the enterprise, could hardy repudiate all responsibility in the matter. If it is wrong to get money by keeping a gaming-saloon, it is also wrong to lend money to some one else so as to enable him to do so.

But such a case is a mere fancy illustration; in most cases when a Government borrows, it borrows for some specific object which is quite unexceptionable, like the laying of a railway or other public works; or it borrows for what may be called general purposes, in order to continue to rule. In the latter case the ethical question is not simply, Shall I enable this Government to do some particular thing which my conscience condemns? but, Shall I enable this Government to exist? and, Can I trust it not to do more harm than good with the resources with which I supply it? Even if after-events show that the money was misused, and the schemes of the statesmen utterly miscarry, it may not be easy to blame him, still less to blame those who enabled him to attempt it. We may take the case that has roused most criticism against bondholders—the case of Egypt. Granting that the Government of Egypt has been in many ways extravagant and bad, and that the pressure of debt was so heavy as to be almost intolerable, and recognising all the complications which the attempt to protect the bondholders' interests has brought about, we may still remember that Mr. Stanley, looking back over all the ghastly failure, yet speaks with enthusiasm of the great attempt to found a widely extended Egyptian empire. It is difficult to say that those who furnished the resources for that enterprise were to blame for enabling Ismail to make the attempt.

After all, a bad Government is better than none ; it is very unlikely that any Government which has credit to borrow is so bad, so certain to use its resources cruelly and oppressively, that it is wrong to supply it with resources. The precise manner in which the loan is used, and the precise results which follow from such expenditure, cannot be definitely foreseen. There is the element of uncertainty about this which renders all questions of practical politics so fascinating to some minds, and so uninteresting to others. We never can tell exactly how the matter will turn out, and there is an element of speculation about the whole affair. While a man would not be excusable who lent money that he knew would be misused, there are few who would hesitate to lend to a Government for fear that that body should misuse it, or who, if the money was squandered or worse, would feel that they ought to have foreseen it and were personally to blame.

(*c*) The case of lending to a private person is not dissimilar. If it is clear that if the money is going to be used for a particular purpose of which the lender disapproves, he is not justified in making the loan. And this may apply to other cases than money used for immoral purposes. If a man burdens his estate not in order to enable him to make

permanent improvements, but in order to maintain an extravagant expenditure, he is at least acting foolishly, and it
is wrong to help him to make a fool of himself. The lender
can probably make such enquiries without much trouble
as will enable him to satisfy himself on this point. The fact
that the borrower wants the money because he likes living
extravagantly, and that he is willing to pay for it, or that
he will get it easily enough from someone if I refuse, does
not acquit me of my responsibility for supplying the loan.
I am to blame if I knowingly abet him in continuing in an
extravagant career, and in nine cases out of ten the enquiries
which are made as to the value of the security offered will
bring out the character of the borrower.

2. There are many cases, however, where a man manages
his capital himself, or chooses the direction in which he will
invest it. He does not lend it, but he enters into business
on his own account, or he becomes a partner by buying
shares; if that business is immoral or mischievous he is to
blame. That someone else might engage in it if he did not
does not alter the case; the question is as to my personal
duty with my information and as I judge of the influence of
a certain enterprise. I am not called to condemn another for
doing what I feel to be wrong for me—so long as society per-
mits it—but still less am I at liberty to correct my conscientious
conviction by appealing to the practice of these people.

(*a*) In regard to every sort of industrial enterprise which
is allowed by English public opinion, it may be said that it
is not wrong in itself, but that blame may arise because
of the habitual misuse of the articles produced, and which
might be used innocently. Is the producer to blame for
wrong done by the man who purchases the article? Is
the wrong in making it, or in misusing it when it is made?
The distinction may be illustrated by an extreme case, such
as the alleged manufacture in Birmingham of idols for export
to India. The 'idol is nothing;' the manufacture of an ugly
image of an impossible monster is not wrong; to manufacture
similar articles for nicknacks in drawing-rooms would be
catering for a harmless taste for grotesques; the mischief

lies in the wrong use of a material object,—in the idolatry. At the same time, there can be so little doubt that the idols will be used in connexion with heathen rites, that those who manufacture them must be aware that they are aiding and abetting in idolatrous worship. Where there is practically speaking no 'use' for an article except one that is wicked, the manufacturer of that article is more blameworthy than the man who ignorantly worships it.

(*b*) We might take an opposite case; there may be a publisher who devotes large sums to the translation and publication of Christian writings, in the belief that a real service is done to religion by disseminating such literature, and he may find it a profitable enterprise. But in the descriptions in which the fathers occasionally indulged of pagan society and denunciations of pagan vices there is a great deal of plain speaking on gross subjects. He might find that portions of the works he had published were susceptible of great abuse, and had, as a matter of fact, pandered to the depraved tastes of vicious persons. How far is he to be blamed for this misuse of an article which he has produced with the best intentions? In such a case it may be possible to guard against the misuse by excisions; but the illustration may at all events serve to bring out the point of the difficulty.

3. There is no material object which is bad in itself; it only becomes an evil if it is badly used. The root of the evil lies not in making the thing, but in the wrong use of the thing; but for all that, the scrupulous man cannot disclaim responsibility for manufacturing articles which are persistently and habitually misused, because he cannot but be aware that he is pandering to probable misuse.

(*a*) There is one business which is carried on in this country on a very large scale about which this question has come to be of practical importance—the brewing trade. It is of course obvious that good beer is a good thing; and there is no question here of bad beer or of adulteration, or of dishonest trade, but only of the manufacture of a good article which is in itself harmless. On the other hand, it is clear that in this country there are many persons who misuse beer, and that a considerable portion of brewers' profits must be due to sale which takes place not in connexion with the temperate use, but in connexion with the intemperate misuse of beer. This is so generally recognised that in one constituency recently the voters insisted that their member should cease to hold brewery shares; they did not wish to be represented by a man who derived profit from a business which they regarded as not above suspicion; and it is also rumoured that this feeling has led to differences of opinion among the partners, and alterations in the constitution of at least one great firm of brewers.

(*b*) Inasmuch as beer has a legitimate use, brewing is a perfectly legitimate business which is in itself thoroughly unexceptionable and honourable, like any other industrial undertaking; that need not be a matter of argument, though there are Manichaeans who would contest it. At the same time the personal responsibility of the brewer, as a man, does not necessarily end when the article is produced; he cannot altogether disregard the manner in which the article is consumed, for it is by the consumption of his beer that his capital is replaced, and that his profit accrues. In so far as he is careless whether his beer is misused or not, and in so far as he pushes his business and tries to enlarge the sale without thought of the possibility of abuse, he is shirking a responsibility. In so far as he is aware that his beer is commonly misused, and carries on a business so that he deliberately derives gain from the misuse of beer, he is certainly to blame. But it is very difficult to carry on this particular kind of business in the present condition of this country without falling into mischief of some kind. The attempt to push a sale by taking up the retail trade is apt to tend to abuse, for it is very difficult to exercise an effective supervision over houses that are thus managed. It may therefore be said of brewing that it is a kind of business which is perfectly legitimate but which it is particularly difficult to conduct without incurring the guilt of gaining through the vices of others.

Where a man brews in connexion with his own hotel, and exercises a personal supervision over the consumption as well as the sale, he is in the best possible position for preventing abuses; the risk of evil is much greater in the case of large firms, which not only brew for wholesale customers, but own a large number of public-houses for the sale of their beer; in such cases the possibility of effective management, and therefore of avoiding abuses, is reduced. It is still further reduced in the case of breweries which are not managed by private firms, but by companies; the power of each partner in controlling the business is practically nil, while the directors are more tempted than the managers of other firms to push the business with mere regard to possible profit. In the case of brewing the effort of the virtuous man will be to guard against the dangers of misuse, and to avoid as far as may be the deliberate effort to gain because of misuse; and consequently the matter turns very much on the carefulness of the management, and its effectiveness. When the control is personal and effective, the risk of abuse is at a minimum; where responsibility is divided there is great difficulty in exercising a complete control. Thus the question wears a very different aspect in the case of the man who brews for consumption on his own premises, and in that of the man who holds brewery shares, and draws a gain without any consideration for, or any effective power of, preventing possible misuse.

It is of course true that the prevention of abuse in this matter is an affair of social importance, and that no single individual can do much to abate it. He may do his best to guard against mischief in connexion with his own business, but that will do little to alter the habits of society. So far as abuse can be limited by municipal regulation or by legislation, it is incumbent on the good citizen to endeavour to frame measures that will abate the evils of intemperance. It is of course the part of the brewer, as of every other citizen, to promote any measure that would really have this result; but it may be that in aiming at this result some legislative enactment would impose serious restrictions on the brewer's business, and his interest as a trader would conflict with the duty of promoting a measure of general benefit

to the community. In such cases it would call for much
public spirit to join in the attempt to limit the abuse by
legislative means; and there might be at least a temptation
to postpone public duty to private advantage, and to refuse
to take active part in putting down abuses which prove profitable to himself personally. This is a position which the
scrupulous man will wish to avoid; he would be anxious not
to slip into a position where his personal and pecuniary
interest might tempt him to be lukewarm, or even to oppose
a well-considered measure for checking the evil of intemperance.

The business of brewing may be taken as typical of other
cases, and the discussion may be summed up in a general
form. Any business which is in itself useful and honourable
offers a legitimate employment for capital; but when the
products of the business are frequently misused, and when
the profits of the business arise, in part at least, from the
misuse of the article manufactured, it is incumbent on the
manufacturer not to ignore the misuse and deny his responsibility, but to endeavour to take precautions against misuse.
It is very difficult to take precautions if a business is being
developed rapidly, and very difficult to carry them out where
the organisation is large and complicated. There may also
be a conflict between private interest and public duty as a
citizen, and the scrupulous man will wish to avoid placing
himself in a position where it is so difficult to act with recti-
tude. Rather than be liable to slip into the position of
abetting intemperance, and gaining through the vices of others,
he will prefer to eschew that calling altogether.

4. One solution of the difficulty for which there is a good
deal to be said is that a trade of this kind should be a Government monopoly. This may appear paradoxical, as it has
just been remarked that effective control will give the best
safeguard against abuses; and it is notorious, as has been
pointed out above, that Government administration is apt to
be lax. This is true; but it is also true that the Government
need not push the business for the sake of profit, or in order
to compete with other traders, and that by possessing the

complete control it may be able to limit the supply. This was attempted in England under James I, and it is the practical effect of the high license policy which is in vogue in many of the American States. The State could thus carry on the legitimate business at a large profit, and at the same time devise any possible measures for preventing abuse.

There is, of course, the real difficulty that any arbitrary restrictive measure is likely to offer great temptations to illicit manufacture and secret drinking, and that such practices are exceedingly demoralising; and this is true. Some people urge that it is wrong for the Government to reap a gain from the self-indulgence of the subjects, but this contention seems to involve some misapprehension of the particular case. The point of the whole proposal rests on the belief that the Government can so manipulate their monopoly as to reduce the evil to a minimum; that it can get its profits from the production of a much used national beverage, but that the possession of a monopoly would put the Government in the best possible position for checking incidental abuses. While such a solution might seem to be the best possible, there is no prospect whatever of any attempt to carry it out in this country; and we are therefore left in this position, that while it is a useful and honourable thing to produce good beer, there is yet so much danger of being insensibly led to become a conscious accessory to intemperance and evil, that the scrupulous man will prefer to avoid such an investment unless he is able to exercise a complete control, and believes that he is able to guard effectively against the dangers of misuse.

III. Relinquishing Business in consequence of Conscientious Scruples.

1. But there may be a further difficulty. If a man comes to have scruples about a business in which he is engaged, how is he to get rid of it? There are two possible courses; he may (*a*) shut the whole thing down and sell the plant for its worth as material,—a transaction which must involve serious loss, and may mean absolute ruin. Or (*b*) he may sell the business as a going concern, or his share in the

business to another man who feels no scruple about it, though by so doing he involves another man in the very career which he has himself discarded on conscientious grounds. To incur ruin would be the more heroic course; it might conceivably be the right course if the business were in itself immoral, like keeping a gambling saloon; such a sacrifice would certainly place a man in an effective position for leading a crusade against abuses connected with a trade in itself useful.

2. But though it might be a heroic proceeding it does not appear to be incumbent on the man who has begun to feel conscientious scruples about gaining from a business which is generally recognised as allowable and honourable. It is wrong for him, with his conviction as to its bearing, and his felt difficulty to prevent abuses; but it may not be wrong for another. He has a perfect right to realise his capital and sell a business which he does not desire to manage and does not wish to push. His withdrawing from the trade would in any case make room for others to enter, or to enlarge their business. If he shuts down, the neighbouring brewers will be the gainers, and he will lose heavily, but there will be no diminution of the supply to the public. If he sells, he carries his money out of the trade, and a new man enters on the field. The practical bearing of his deciding to take the heroic course is that in one case he loses and his competitors gain; in the other case he severs his connexion with the trade, and competition continues as before. In such a case it seems that a man who scrupled to hold a property need have no scruple about selling it; his personal feeling makes it wrong for him to continue to profit by it; but his personal feeling gives him no right to condemn all those who are carrying on a business which society regards as allowable and useful.

3. There is another matter about which difficulty is felt. Supposing a man comes to have scruples about the way in which his money has been acquired, how far is he justified in continuing to enjoy it? For example, a fortune may have been made originally by dealing in slaves; that is an im-

moral business; and we can easily suppose a case where the grandson of a Liverpoo or Bristol merchant enjoys an estate or a fortune which was notoriously acquired by a mode of business which is now illegal.

(*a*) So far as the man who has inherited such a fortune is concerned, it may be said that he has himself come honestly by it; that it has descended to him, and that he has had no part in the doubtful transactions by which it was acquired at first. Since the property has come into his hands, his main duty would appear to be the conscientious discharge of his obligations as a proprietor; he ought to be careful, as all other proprietors should, about the manner in which he uses his property. If there is a possibility of restitution and reparation to any who have been wronged it is an undoubted duty to make it; but when reparation is no longer possible, there does not seem to be any obligation for me to pay Paul because Peter has been robbed by my grandfather. But the whole matter wears a different aspect with regard to the personal enjoyment of gains which a man has himself acquired by unscrupulous conduct. There is a far clearer call and probably a far greater opportunity for restitution and for attempts at reparation, and no man can have a moral right to enjoy what he was not justified in acquiring.

(*b*) Even so, however, there is a very great distinction between gain which was acquired by dishonesty and chicanery, that was known to be dishonourable at the time, and gain which accrued through a business which was pursued in all good faith and with a clear conscience, but which has come to be differently regarded through the gradual elevation of public sentiment, as slave-dealing has. In the latter case the attempt at reparation would be a voluntary act, which the scrupulous man might feel it right to do; in the former there would be an equitable claim which might possibly be enforced in law even after the lapse of many years. But the most important questions in regard to money are not as to the means by which it has been originally acquired, but as to the manner in which it should be used; and to this we must return later.

CHAPTER XIII.

Duty in regard to the Return on Capital.

It is usual to distinguish the return which the capitalist receives into three parts: Interest, Insurance against Risk, and Wages of Management. This analysis is very unsatisfactory in each of its parts, but nothing better can be expected so long as only one form of capital is taken into account, and the subject is treated as if all capital were employed in industry, and administered by the man who owns it. If we wish to discuss what is right and wrong in regard to the return on capital we must include all capital, whether engaged in industry or not; and we must analyse the return which accrues, not on one form only, but on all forms of capital.

I. Wages of Management.

1. There is indeed one part of the employers' receipts which cannot be properly included as part of his profit, and which recent economists have rightly considered under an entirely different head. This is the element termed Wages of Management. It is plainly distinct even in connexion with capital employed in industry, for in a Joint Stock Company the owners of the capital will for the most part take no effective part in the management, and the wages of management will be paid to men who do not own any part of the capital. Thus in a Railway Company, the shareholders and debenture-holders own the capital, but they take no real part in the management; some of them do not even familiarise

themselves with the half-yearly reports, and few of them ever attend the meetings or send proxies, unless on some very unusual occasion, and after an active whip for their suffrages. Wages of superintendence and management are paid to numerous officials, from the general manager with some thousands a year, down to the foreman porter at thirty shillings a week; and of those who draw wages of management as responsible servants, none need be shareholders, and probably very few, if any, are shareholders, or have any part of the profits. The only persons who draw both are the chairman and directors; they are, on one hand, partners, and partners with considerable shares; and, on the other hand, they draw fees for attendance at meetings, and thus obtain wages for their services. But on the whole it is true to say that the shareholders get profits, but no wages of management; and on the other that the responsible servants get wages for managing the concern, but draw no profits. Such a case brings out the impossibility of drawing a line between wages of superintendence and wages for labour. The foreman porter when he is directing other men is superintending and managing; but when he is himself handling luggage or screwing up a coupling, he is labouring. The interconnexion is still closer in office work; at one time a clerk is writing invoices which are necessary for the safe and regular conveyance of goods, at another he is checking returns; in the one case he may be said to be working at the business of the company, in the other to be superintending and checking the work of others. We cannot distinguish them as manual labour and head work, nor as responsible and mechanical employment, for the driver of an engine is in a very responsible position, and yet he is doing work, not superintending the work of others. We cannot distinguish the one kind of service from the other; though it may serve to classify them by the manner in which they are commonly paid, and to say that those who labour are paid weekly wages and those who superintend are paid quarterly salaries. This is a very crude way of dividing the groups of workers and superintendents; but the different modes of remuneration roughly correspond to different kinds of service, and may be taken as representing the two classes of servants.

2. For though there is such difficulty in classifying the different grades of service, the fact that there are such different grades is of the highest importance. Superintendence and management, what may be called responsible service, is sometimes remunerated on a very liberal scale, and there are not wanting signs that the labourer is inclined to view these large payments with some little jealousy. Thus, when some years ago the Midland Railway reduced the payments to a very large number of their servants, there was much dissatisfaction expressed because the 'gold-lace officials' suffered little if any diminution. It is also said that in working men's co-operative societies, the salaries of the high officials are by no means so large as in similar businesses conducted as private firms. In distributive societies they possibly do not need so much business capacity as firms that rely on competition, and the comparative failure in productive enterprise may possibly be partly due to neglect of this factor in success. It is quite possible that enterprise, shrewdness, and complete trustworthiness are qualities which the employer finds it well worth while to pay for; that the example of heads of departments influences all their subordinates, and that it is prudent for capitalists to pay almost any sum to secure or to retain the services of a thoroughly good man as a superintendent. In fact, it appears that if it were not worth while it would not be done. But the important point remains that these large salaries are paid as wages and for services, and that they are in no sense paid to a man as a return on his capital.

3. It has been necessary to go into this at some length in order to enforce the proposition that, when we are considering the return on capital, the wages of management must be rigorously excluded; and that in the case of those who themselves manage the business in which capital is invested a very large allowance must be made for the amount they are entitled to as wages for their successful management. It is easy to contrast the style in which the owner of a cotton mill

lives with that of his hands; he has a handsome house, and sends his boys to a public school, while the hands live in a tenement, and may often have difficulty about threepenny fees. But a very similar contrast might be drawn between the manager of a bank or an insurance company and one of the copying clerks. The company pays the man of business-capacity handsomely, while the man who does mere drudgery has to manage on a mere pittance. It may be true that there is unfairness in the apportionment of wages for different classes of service, but this is an entirely distinct question from that of fairness in the apportionment between capital and labour. We want to discriminate the employer as capitalist from the employer as the energetic man of business; and we are only called upon at present to consider the gain which accrues to him in the former capacity.

II. How the Return on Capital is obtained.

If, then, we exclude the wages of management, and take account of capital in all its various forms, we shall find that there are two sources from which the gain is ultimately derived—(*a*) on the one hand, it is obtained by securing a right to levy taxes, and (*b*) on the other hand, it is derived from success in catering for the wants of the public. It is here that the distinction to which allusion has been so frequently made between capital that is lent and capital that is employed in business comes into clear light. The man who lends money at interest bargains for the right to draw on the resources of the borrower; if he lends to a nation he expects to be paid annually out of the proceeds of the taxes; if he lends to a municipality he expects to be paid annually by means of the rates; if he lends on mortgage to a land-owner, he expects to be able to obtain payment regularly out of the rental. It does not matter to him whether the nation or the city or the landlord use his money in a re-munerative manner or not. They may employ it profitably, or they may expend it in display; it is all the same to him, so long as they are able respectively to fulfil their obligations.

They may use his money unproductively—whether usefully or not—or they may use it in a productive enterprise which proves a complete failure ; but so long as it does not involve the borrower in ruin, the lender's claim holds good, and is unaffected by the misjudgment of the borrower.   For in such cases the lender counts to gain by his *right to tax the resources of the borrower*, and this definite right remains.

On the other hand, he may gain by success in catering for a public want; he enters into business, and supplies goods which the public buy, so that he replaces his capital at a profit.   If business is good, his profit may be very large ; if it falls off he may merely replace his capital, or he may be forced to work for a time at an absolute loss.   But whether profit is high or not it is always varying—as business itself fluctuates,—sometimes high, sometimes low, and sometimes disappearing altogether; it can never be definitely calculated upon, and sometimes it does not accrue at all.   This is the marked difference between the return which is paid on loans, and the return which is obtained by capital employed in business.   The lender bargains for a definite rate of return, and bargains to receive it for certain; the borrower's bankruptcy may deprive him both of principal and interest, and he is forced to take that risk; but by the terms of his bargain, and so long as the borrower can pay his way at all, the lender insists on a definite rate of return, and on having it paid without fail.   The man in business is in a very different position; his gain is contingent, for he may not get any, and he cannot generally expect that any two years will be exactly alike ; the second may be better or it may be worse, but it will not probably be precisely the same as the first. The one man counts to gain by taxation, and he can bargain for a definite rate of return at stated times; but the gain of the other is necessarily contingent, as it accrues in the course of trade, and is affected by fluctuations of every kind.

(A) 1. The man who lends his money to a Government renders a very real service.   This has never been denied.   What has been maintained was that this was a service for which it was impossible to assess the fair remuneration, and that therefore it should be done out of charity, if at all, as any demand for remuneration tended dangerously towards extortion. Public opinion and the law of the land alike agree at present in regarding bargains of this sort as allowable. The mere fact that borrowing offers the easiest means to any Government for procuring the use of capital—that it is in its superior facilities for borrowing that Government has an advantage over private capitalists or associations—makes it clear that the wise states-man may wish to borrow. He may intend to start public works which will prove remunerative, either directly or indi-rectly; or he may have some scheme of educational improve-ment which involves a large outlay, and this can be most easily met by borrowing. The public works, like a railway, may prove remunerative directly; public works, like a har-bour, may facilitate commerce, and be remunerative indi-rectly; public expenditure on education may be beneficial to the inhabitants, and thus bring about in the more or less distant future an improvement in that most important element of national resources—the population. By aiding in any of these the lender does a service, and it is a service for which he may fairly claim compensation in money. The question of personal duty then will arise in this shape, Whether it is possible to discriminate between a fair and unfair rate of return for a loan? and Whether it is possible to guard against the danger of falling insensibly into extortion in connexion with such gains?

2. At the same time the fact that there is a need which the lender supplies can at least only give a justification for paying something; it does not at all help us to understand how much it is fair to pay. The lender is put to some trouble, or risk, or privation, in making the loan; but how much compensation is adequate? He may fairly claim to receive enough to com-pensate him, and the difficulty is to estimate the fair compen-sation. But there is always the danger of looking at it from the other side, of estimating the service rendered by the need of the borrower, and being satisfied to take whatever he is willing to pay. Now it is obvious that the greater the man's need is, the more he will pay rather than fail to get the

accommodation; and that the more necessitous a man's circumstances, the greater is the rate which he will offer. This is equally true whether it is the temporary embarrassment of a rich man, or the last chance of an insolvent. In this latter case the risk would be great, and the lender might fairly ask for the promise of large compensation if he consented to undertake the risk. But the temporary embarrassment of a rich man may not mean that there is real risk in lending him money; and it is tempting to measure the charge by what he can afford, or what he is ready to give, and not by what it costs the lender in privation and anxiety to meet this need. Wherever the rate of return is based on the necessities of the borrower, and not on the cost to the lender, there is real extortion; for the lender gains by trading on the necessities of another.

3. If it is not easy to discriminate in any single case, and to make sure that in the rate agreed on the lender has not taken advantage of the needs of the borrower, it is obviously impossible to get any help from examining a number of such cases and considering the market for loans. For there may be a number of eager and necessitous borrowers; colonial governments anxious to attract emigrants, and indulging in costly harbour works and railways; municipalities laying out parks or building libraries; any of them may be terribly reckless in burdening posterity so as to defray present expenditure. If the rate of interest obtainable rises, it may only show that there are more people anxious to borrow, or that the borrowers are more anxious for accommodation. And by floating such schemes the responsible authorities may be burdening a community with a heavy debt, which requires very heavy taxation in order to defray the interest. The market for capital only shows what the borrower on good security is, as a matter of fact, ready to give; it does not show for certain what is adequate compensation to the lender.

4. There may, as a matter of fact, be extortion in exacting the interest agreed on in connexion with Government loans. There is such a thing as a limit of profitable taxation, and if the burden imposed by borrowing were such that the limit of

profitable taxation had been passed, and the country was becoming more and more exhausted annually in order to meet the demands of foreign creditors, there would be real extortion; and there might be serious distress before the pressure became so serious. The precise object for which the money was borrowed is not of importance; it may have been for public works which did not prove remunerative, or for great institutions which the country could not afford. Where the fault lay, or whether the loss was due to unforeseen circumstances, does not matter; if a burden of interest is pressing so heavily on a country as to exhaust it, there is extortion in continuing to collect the taxation which is needed in order to meet the demands of the lenders; and it is most desirable on every account that relief should be given in some form or other.

There are two countries at present where the pressure of public indebtedness is very severely felt; different in the forms of government, in the climate and productions and everything else, but alike in suffering from a burden of debt which retards progress, even if it does not positively exhaust. In New Zealand and in Egypt alike there was a period of rapid borrowing on account of schemes which have not met the expectations of those who brought them forward. Such a state of affairs is recognised by law and public opinion, and to repudiate the debt would be dishonest; if a nation has made a bad bargain it is a crime to attempt to evade it, or to confiscate the property of men whose only crime is that they have placed confidence in a national promise. At the same time the scrupulous man might prefer not to be placed in such a position; he might dislike to feel that his income was wrung from starving felaheen. If so, his remedy is an easy one—he will avoid subscribing to Government loans unless the country is so rich, or the rate of interest is so low, that there is no appreciable risk that the pressure of taxation to meet the interest due to him will be a serious burden.

5. There is, however, another way in which the remuneration received by the lender may become excessive, as he or his descendants may profit through a national necessity. In

the time of the French wars, Pitt was obliged to borrow on
terms which were high even then, and were ludicrously out
of proportion to the rate which is current at the present
time.   The greater part of the national debt has been so
financed that these anomalies are done away with; but there
were many years when the nation continued to pay terminable
annuities or tontines at a most extravagant rate.   Here it
may be felt that the nation made the bargain with its eyes
open, that as it was able to meet it there was an obligation
to abide by it, and that there was no call on the part of the
fortunate creditors to offer to be satisfied with less.   There
certainly was not; but at the same time it may be felt that
they were lucky dogs who were able to make an exceedingly
good thing out of their bargain.   Attention is called to it
here, because it reveals a criterion which we do occasionally
apply and which does give a good test of the cost to the
lender in making an advance.   We feel that these men who
drew their 7 or 10 per cent. were excessively fortunate,
because the average rate of return which might be reaped by
contingent profits had come to be so much lower.   If the
capitalist who carried on a trade could only average, apart
from wages of management, 5 per cent., and the Government
creditor was drawing 6 per cent. or 7 per cent., then he was
getting a return which was felt to be excessive.   And this is
a sound criterion; the ordinary rate of profit in any country
serves to give an indication as to a fair rate of interest,
for it gives a measure that is simply based on the cost to the
lender and has no reference to the need of the borrower.
The lender can obtain the ordinary rate of business profit, if
he invests in railway stock; he has at least a right to be compensated for the gain he sacrifices by not investing in an enterprise of the sort, and he may certainly claim *lucrum cessans*.
But as the payment of any profit from a business—and at all
events the rates of profit—are contingent, he may well be
satisfied with less than the average rate of profit when he is
going to get a regular return at a definite rate.   On the
other hand, if there is a more serious risk in lending on
inferior security, he may demand more than the average

rate of profit. so as to include insurance; because he is really risking his principal—*periculum sortis*. The average rate of business profit, that is of contingent return, gives a criterion as to the cost and privation for which the lender can fairly claim compensation; though the element of less or greater risk must also be taken into account before it can be satisfactorily applied.

6. The best criterion we can get for fair interest on a loan is found by comparing it with the average rate of profit from ordinary enterprise. It is likely to be free from extortion, for if the loan is sensibly applied to remunerative public works or to developing the resources of the country and the nation, it ought to be possible to earn this rate of return at least, so that the Government need not be out of pocket in paying the interest on its debt. Even if it borrows for unproductive expenditure like a war, the lender can satisfy himself or anyone else that his demand was not excessive. The profit obtained in business is entirely different in character from the gain that accrues by lending; the lender's gain arises from the fact that he has acquired a right to tax, and the man who carries on a business in the face of competition has neither the power nor the right to tax. But although they are so different, they are not entirely unconnected, as the capitalist may choose to obtain gain either in one fashion or the other, and the man who is only compensated for gain he might have had by trading, with due allowance for risk, has not asked an excessive rate.

(B) 1. The return which accrues to the man who is engaged in business comes from separate and distinct transactions, some of which may be more successful and others less. Some branch of the business may hardly pay, but it may be worth while to keep it going in order to avoid waste, or because it leads to remunerative business. Thus it is commonly said that the grocer makes little or no profit on sugar, but finds it worth while to deal in it, so that customers may not go elsewhere for their tea. And so in manufacturing; one order may be turned out at a handsome profit, another at little better than a loss, or the works may be almost idle for weeks, and the profit on months of hard work may be absorbed in keeping things together. In building operations undertaken on a contract which runs on for several months or years, there may be changes in the rates for material or wages which will render the whole work highly profitable or very much the reverse. There is no regular rate of return and therefore there can hardly be a question as to a fair rate of return. We may strike an average of the transactions in a given period as they have occurred in all sorts of different businesses, and thus get an average rate of profit for that time ; we may expect that the average rate for some months in the future will be higher or lower than in the past, but there is no regular rate ; there is sometimes a big haul and sometimes a little one, as in the herring fishery ; but there is no regular and constant rate at all, because the whole gain is contingent. The ethical question must present itself in a different shape from that we have considered, and we must not ask, What is a fair rate? but, What is a fair division of the produce?

2. Labour and Capital are the two factors interested in the division, and the employer who manages the business is the agent in the division. In putting the matter in this way we need not forget that there are many persons who hold that there should be no such division, but that the whole produce should go to labour. No industry can be carried on without labour ; that is true, labour is a necessary element in all production. But labour is not the sole agent in production ; the strength of purpose which hoards and the enterprise which uses a hoard are elements which bring the great forces of nature into play, so that human strength and skill may be to some extent assisted, and to some extent superseded. From all that has been said on the formation of capital, and on its effectiveness when formed, it seems to follow that the capitalist has a claim to some share in the product.

3. We may first look at the division of the gross produce, that is of the total amount which is realised by the sale of the product. It is obvious that this amount will vary accord-

ing as trade is good or bad; it is also certain that for many purposes these fluctuations are an evil, though owing to the superior fluidity of capital, the capitalist can adapt himself to them and take advantage of them more easily than the labourer. But so long as these fluctuations continue there must be variations in the amount of the gross produce and in the sum which can be divided. On the whole, too, it seems that the only fair principle is, that the division of the produce should be according to the relative importance of each factor in production. That is to say, if any business requires £5000 to buy the materials and to keep up the buildings and plant, and £5000 to feed and maintain the men in good condition, the labourers might claim half the produce; while if it required £9000 to buy materials and maintain the building and plant, and £1000 for wages, the labourers would only be justified, on the same principle, in claiming one-tenth of the product. Now, in by far the greater number of industrial employments during the last hundred years there has been an immense increase of machinery, and the relative importance of labour as a factor in production has been greatly reduced; this has been pointed out above in a different connexion. It therefore follows that there must be a general depression of labour relatively to capital in the division of the gross produce; and that of the total wealth produced a relatively larger share will go to capital, and a relatively smaller share will go to labour. That this has been the case is patent to all, and is matter of common remark; the division between the rich and the poor is far more marked than it was; the long streets of immense mansions in London, of villas in the suburbs, or the great residential towns at the seaside, tell of a very numerous *rentier* class, and it is a matter of common belief that most of the middle classes, including retail shop-keepers, live in greater comfort than the corresponding classes in the last generation. About this there is no dispute; on the other hand, the question as to whether the wage-earners, skilled and unskilled alike, organised and un-organised, have gained or not by the changes of the last fifty

years, is hotly debated.   There certainly is a good deal of
evidence which goes to show that there has been a relative
depression of the labourer as compared with the capitalist,
and that the labourer has not enjoyed such a large pro-
portional share in the increased wealth of England in 1890,
as he enjoyed of the comparatively small amount of wealth
produced in 1800.   Considered as a question of honest
bargaining we might ask, How could he?   He does relatively
less.   Considered as a question, not of generosity, but of
justice, we might ask, Why should he, since he does relatively
less as a factor in production?   Why should he continue to
share in the same proportion as before?   From all which it
appears that it is not easy to get to close quarters with the
right and wrong in regard to this division unless we look at
the matter in some detail, and do not content ourselves with
stating a broad principle of justice.

4. We may therefore consider the division which the
capitalist makes as a matter of practice.   There is constant
outlay required to continue his business as a going concern;
there is (*a*) an outlay on machinery and materials, and also
(*b*) an outlay on wages, including salaries; with the former he
maintains his plant, with the latter his labourers; (*c*) the difference between his outlay and his receipts by the sale of the
produce is profit, and this he retains as remuneration for the
capital employed.   There is, taking the average of any period
of years, a minimum rate which is necessary to induce him to
continue in that business; if he conducts his business well,
or is specially fortunate, he may get much more, but he will
be unwilling to take less.   He may submit for a long time to
a very low return rather than attempt to realise and remove
his capital; it is impossible to state in general terms the
amount of success which he must have in order to be tempted
to continue, but unless he thinks he can work at some sort of
a profit, and be remunerated for incurring the risks and
anxiety of the business, he will not engage in it, or will not
voluntarily remain in it.   This may be called the *necessary
remuneration of enterprise*, as unless there is reason to expect
such a return the enterprise will not be forthcoming; but it

may vary immensely in different places, or in the same place at different times. But we are able to find a rough indication of this necessary remuneration by looking at one kind of enterprise; there are particular advantages in rural employments which render them attractive to many men, and there are not such sudden fluctuations as in many other employments, even if we do not allow anything for superintendence. The rate of return which a man expects to get when he uses his capital as a farmer, or the rate of return which a moneyed man expects to get when he sinks his capital in land and buys an estate, may be taken as helping to indicate the remuneration which is necessary in order to induce a man to go on with any kind of business.

(i) This necessary amount will, of course, vary according to different social conditions—political security and the like. In countries where there is a great deal of available capital people will be forced by competition to be content with a smaller inducement than in new lands where capital is much wanted for many purposes. But on the whole the return that is obtained by working land, or by the man who sinks his capital in purchasing an estate, may be taken as an index to the remuneration of capital that is necessary, there and then, if the owner is to enter or to continue to follow any form of enterprise. It is, of course, only an index, as there must be an allowance for greater risk, either physical or commercial, and less attractiveness, perhaps, in various other employments; and the necessary remuneration for capital in manufacturing gunpowder, or in weaving cloth, at any place and time, may probably be explained by some such allowances on the basis of the rate indicated by the return from land, but will not be identical with it.

If the capitalist does not, on an average, earn this necessary rate of remuneration over any period, he will withdraw from the business, and in so far as the same thing occurs in the trade generally, that industry will decline, and perhaps decay altogether in that district. This entails a great waste of capital, but, as has been noted above, it involves far more serious and irreparable loss to the labourers. They cannot find employment at once, they may not be able to find it at all without emigrating, and a period of idleness, even if it does not necessitate a change of abode, must be a serious drain on the savings of years, if it does not plunge the man hopelessly in debt. There can be no more serious evil to the labourers in any employment than that the master's capital should fail to receive the necessary remuneration, and that the works should be closed in consequence.

(ii) This necessary rate, then, gives the minimum which the owner must receive, on an average, of his transactions over any period, to induce him to continue in his enterprise; and, of course, the profits on particular transactions will often be very much larger than the 'necessary rate.' In times of good trade they will exceed the necessary rate on every transaction for a longer or shorter period, and in cases where a man has a trade secret, whether protected by patent or not, or has any other means of defying competition—as by agreeing with all possible competitors—the profits may be very large indeed. But wherever competition is in effective operation no manufacturer can hope to enjoy exceptional profits for long, as the action of other competitors, and their efforts to undersell him and get a footing in the trade, will force him to diminish his prices, and thus to leave a smaller margin between his outlay and the value of the product.

Exceptional profit, secured by agreement, is a phenomenon that is attracting much attention in the United States, where rings and trusts have been formed in a fashion that is unknown in this country; in it we notice the reappearance, under new conditions, of the evils which mediaeval legislators attempted to prevent when they legislated against engrossers and forestallers. When such schemes are worked successfully manufacturers are able to gain at the expense of the public, instead of merely gaining because they have succeeded in serving the public; there is no justification for such gains, though in some cases the public are quite as well and cheaply served by the monopolists as they could hope to be by competing traders. But an exceptional profit which arises temporarily or incidentally in a trade which is subject to competition is not likely to do much more than reimburse the capitalist for periods when he did not even receive the necessary amount of remuneration, but continued to work at a positive loss in the hope that trade would mend.

5. There are many schemes in the present day for effecting a more equal division of profits, or for enabling the labourer to participate in profits.

(*a*) In so far as the necessary remuneration of the capitalist goes, it is not possible to reduce it and pay any portion away; the labourer can only share in this if he is an owner of some part of the capital, and there is a scheme for *industrial partnership*. There are, however, some grave practical objections to industrial partnership in any of the forms in which it has been tried in this country. It implies that the labourer shall invest all his savings in a given enterprise, and in the enterprise to which he looks for the payment of his wages. If, owing to any new invention or other change, the business should cease to pay and should ultimately fail, the labourer will be cast on the world, and the very same disaster which throws him out of employment will swallow up all his savings. A prudent man may well desire some other form of investment. But apart from this there may be considerable difficulty in framing a working constitution so that the labourers with small shares and the large shareholders shall be duly represented and have complete confidence in the management. If industrial partnership can be worked out in a satisfactory form it would enable the labourers to share in the necessary remuneration, and give them a portion of the exceptional profit as well.

(*b*) There is less difficulty in framing a scheme which shall first secure to the capitalist the necessary remuneration, and shall afterwards pay a portion of any exceptional profits to the labourers as a *bonus*. This may often serve as a means of obtaining exceptional profits, as the stimulus it gives may enable the partners to dispense with the payment of heavy salaries for superintendence; and by rendering the men more eager to work and more careful at their work it may prove very remunerative. But such schemes have occasionally broken down through a want of confidence between the receivers of bonus and their employers. This may obviously break out when the employers assert that there is no exceptional profit, and when the labourers believe that there ought to be a bonus, and that they have worked so hard as to deserve one ; and though it is good that there should be more diligent labour, it is not good that the strain of labour should be greatly increased without a constant, not a spasmodic, increase of wages.

(*c*) On the whole the most practicable scheme for enabling the labourers to share in exceptional profits is one which is as nearly as possible self-acting, and therefore gives the least possible opportunity for dispute. This is attained in those trades where wages are paid according to a sliding scale ; this does not merely give a bonus to the labourer, and does not therefore stimulate to special work ; but it provides a means by which the ordinary wages of the labourer shall be raised at times when trade is good, and thus enables him to get the benefit of those conditions which give rise to exceptional profits. There may be great difficulties in framing a sliding scale, and it will need to be revised from time to time ; but these difficulties have been faced in many trades with great success. This scheme certainly affords the simplest means for the labourer to benefit by improved trade ; it does not offer him any share in the profits, but it forces the capitalist to increase his outlay in wages at the times when his profit is becoming exceptional. It gives the same sort of benefit, but without implying any unusual confidence between the two parties ; and it gives it in a form in which it is most likely to promote the labourer's comfort, and without imposing any new obligation or special strain upon him.

6. If there are periods of exceptional profit, or transactions of exceptional profit, there are also periods when the employer has to exercise the greatest care in order to make any profit and to reap the necessary remuneration which will induce him to continue in the business. Competition is so keen, we may suppose, that he cannot get larger receipts by the sale of the product, and the only saving he can effect is by

looking carefully at his outlay and seeing if he can cut it down.

(*a*) The cost of materials does not lie in his own control, and he cannot alter it; he may have more choice about repairs to his buildings and the keeping up of his plant; but a niggardly expenditure in these directions may prove very false economy. If he saves in petty repairs he may soon find it necessary to spend a large sum in substantial repairs; if he does not introduce new improvements, but is contented to work with old-fashioned machines, he condemns himself to carry on the competition with his rivals on most unequal terms, and he cannot hope to prosper. The one element of outlay which he can reduce without serious damage to his own property is the labour bill; and therefore he is apt to look out for every means of reducing this item of expenditure, either by paying a lower rate of wages, by employing fewer or less skilled hands, or by getting more work out of those whom he does employ. These are the various expedients by which the employer is tempted to grind down the labourer— whether he yields to the temptation or not. The history of the latter part of the last century and the beginning of this seems to show that employers did yield to the temptation in some cases; in fact, it may be doubted, as was stated above, whether they had power to resist it, until they were assisted by legislative interference. In so far as the labourer was ground down, and forced to submit to a lower standard of comfort, there was not merely a relative depression, but an absolute depression of the labourer. Not only was it true that he was a less important factor in production relatively to capital, and that he received a relatively smaller share than capital in the division of the produce, but that he received an absolutely smaller portion of the necessaries and comforts of life, and that he was positively worse off than before.

(*b*) It is necessary to insist on this distinction so as, if possible, to avoid the possibility of confusion. The relative depression of the labourer appears to be inevitable, as human skill adapts physical forces to carry on industrial processes; but since these physical forces are so powerful, and supply the necessaries and comforts of life in such abundance, the labourer may, when the readjustment has taken place and the time of transition is past, find that he enjoys a larger amount of the comforts of life than he did before. He may find that though he gets relatively less, a smaller proportion of the increased total, he gets also absolutely more. The additional production may be so great that a smaller share of the larger sum amounts to more than the larger share of the smaller sum which he formerly enjoyed. It therefore seems possible that, while in the progress of society there has been a gradual depression of the labourer (as a factor in production and as sharing in the produce) relatively to capital, there has still been no depression, but an improvement, in the condition of the labourer absolutely. On the other hand it is contended by socialists, that though this is theoretically possible, it has not occurred in practical life. It is urged that there has been not only relative but absolute depression in the past, and that we may expect not merely continued relative depression, as we certainly may, but continued absolute depression, so long as the present social regime, and capitalistic era, are permitted to continue.

(*c*) While, on the one hand, it is perfectly clear that there have been times, like those of the industrial revolution, when the labourer was forced to submit to absolute depression, it is also clear that there have been cases where the application of machinery to some department of industry is effected without detriment to the labouring classes. For example, the invention of the locomotive has revolutionised the internal carrying trade; it was feared that inns would be ruined, coachmen and guards done away with, and that horse-breeders would be ruined. But the enormous increase of travelling which has arisen in consequence of the facilities which railways offer has called for a far larger amount of labour than was employed before, in the capacity of engine-drivers, guards, and porters. It may even be doubted whether the very occupations which have suffered most have suffered at all; there are certainly far more inns and hotels than ever before; the employment of horses in local traffic and as subsidiary to the railways must be very large. The North Western Railway requires an enormous number of horses, and the excellence of the English cart-horse has not declined since railways came in. There is as much hunting or more than before, and coaching is not extinct. The outlay for labour all round must be immensely greater than it used to be, and the labourer has been greatly benefited by the facilities for cheap travelling. In such a case there has been relative depression, but absolute improvement so far as labour is concerned.

It would be interesting to endeavour to investigate the results accurately in some of the minor employments in which machinery has been recently introduced. How is the condition of seamstresses affected by the sewing-machine? How is the condition of copyists affected by the typewriter? Not of course those who try to compete against it, but those who use it? Far more sewing and far more copying is done. Labour is a smaller factor than before, but is it worse off or not in consequence of the change? We need not pause to consider each particular case, but we may endeavour to examine the course which affairs have taken over a considerable period, and to see how far they tell in favour of either view.

(*c*) Here, then, we are brought to consider a simple matter of fact; has there, on the whole, been an absolute depression of the labourer under the influence of capital? Those who insist that there has, point triumphantly to the fifteenth century and challenge a comparison of the labourer's position then and now. To the fifteenth century, then, let us go; it was a time when capital had been but little formed in England, and when it was chiefly employed in commerce; there was little scope for investing either in agricultural or industrial pursuits—though the weaving trades were an exception. On some points we have sufficient data for instituting a definite comparison, in other cases the data are wanting. The hours of labour of the fifteenth century peasant were very long, as they lasted from five in the morning till half-past seven at night, with intervals which came to about two hours and a half.   There is reason to believe that employment was very irregular, and that the day labourer was idle for half his time, so that even though the rate of day wages was high, when the difference of the value of money is taken into account, the labourer's income was not large.   As to his command over the comforts of life we know that there are many simple luxuries which he could not procure,—tea, coffee, tobacco, oranges; and that he had no access to newspapers or other literature, and no opportunity for travelling. As to the things he could procure we cannot judge correctly of their quality; but from the frequency of the epidemics that visited the country, it is impossible to believe that the labourer was well housed or had wholesome food.   The furniture in the mansion of a city magnate like William Canynge was so simple that it is most unlikely that the peasant had even a bed in his cabin.   When we do not content ourselves with quoting the rates of wages, but try to picture the conditions of life, it appears that rude and laborious as is the agricultural labourer's life to-day, he is not so utterly sunk in sordid drudgery as was his prototype in the fifteenth century.   If we look at the matter since the beginning of the capitalist era we may say that while there can be no doubt that labour has lost its preeminence in production and has been relatively depressed, there is no proof whatever that it has absolutely suffered, and has been permanently ground down by the influence of capital.

While this is true if we look at the conditions of employment, it is equally true if we consider the numbers of the unemployed. There are terrible accounts of the scarcity of work in London in the fifteenth century, and of the violent outbreaks against foreign competition to which it led under Henry VIII.   The evil did not abate, and was greatly increased in the rural districts by the number of enclosures in the sixteenth century. Some idea of the desperate condition of affairs may be gathered from an estimate of the pauperism at a later date, when industry and commerce were reviving, and in a town which was awakening to a career of great prosperity. In Sheffield in the year 1615, out of a population of 2207, there were no fewer than 725 persons who were begging poor; of the remainder, 160 families were so hard pressed that they could not afford to contribute towards the maintenance of the others, but the whole expense had to be defrayed by the contributions of a small body of 100 householders, and these were only artisans, not one of whom could keep a team on his land, while only two had ground enough for a cow. We must remember, too, that in these days there was little or no provision made for the shelter of the poor; that there were no workhouses, that relief was administered with a most grudging hand, and that the able-bodied beggar was treated as a criminal. There can be little doubt that at the opening of the capitalist period, in a rising town, the paupers were infinitely worse treated and were in a far larger proportion to the population than they are at present. Sad as it is that there should be so many paupers and so many unemployed in the present day, there is every reason to believe that the unemployed and the pauper of Tudor times, as well as the employed, were worse off than the corresponding classes to-day.

(*d*) This conclusion, while it may lead us to reject exaggerated statements about the increasing degradation of the labourers, cannot be regarded as at all satisfactory; for it seems that while the wealth of the country has so largely increased the labourer has not shared greatly, if at all, in the gain. But can this sad result be ascribed to the action of capital? Is it clear that capitalists could have prevented it? In comparing the two periods we must remember that there has been an enormous increase in population; that the present population of England is six or seven times what it was in the fifteenth century. The labourer's standard of comfort has not been raised, and the population has increased to almost the full extent which our increased power over the means of production allows. The labouring classes in their millions receive far more than the thousands of labourers did before the era of capital commenced; but they accept the traditional standard of comfort, and by rapid multiplication the successive opportunities for raising the standard have been lost. It thus appears that we can completely account for the sad fact that the labourer has so little additional comfort, without for a moment supposing that he has been steadily ground down. If the standard of comfort had obviously declined we could not attribute the change to the force of population, but should have to look for the explanation in the oppressive action of capitalists; but where the complaint is that the standard of comfort is so little raised we do not need to seek any more remote cause, but can explain it by saying that the increase of population has gone on so fast as to absorb the opportunities of improved comfort which the labourer might have enjoyed. When this is taken into account we may say with some confidence that there is no proof whatever that capital has exercised a steady influence in grinding down the labourer; he has been but little raised, but he has not been steadily degraded. There is therefore no reason to anticipate that the grinding down will continue, especially when we remember that the cases which appear to give most justification for this fear occurred under social conditions of a very unusual character, and which have long since passed away.

(*e*) At the same time it must not be forgotten that there is real danger of grinding down the labourer, and that there is constant need to be on the guard against it. Organisations of labourers to maintain their own interest in this matter are the most effective weapons, but it does not merely concern the operative classes. It concerns the nation as a whole; just as it is short-sighted of a capitalist to allow his buildings and plant to fall into bad repair, so it is short-sighted of a nation to allow the labouring class to be reduced to a worse condition of mind. Any pressure which threatens to weaken or degrade them is to be resisted by the legislature, and possibly can be resisted in no other way. Such interference is not really pauperising if it improves the conditions of work, and so benefits the worker without affecting the idler. There is more ground for anxiety lest the diminution of hours or increased rates of pay should have a disastrous effect on the position of this country as a competitor with other countries in foreign markets. But if the interference is really called for to prevent the weakening and degrading of the labourer there need be no cause for alarm; the danger really lies the other way, lest our population should be so weakened and enervated that it could not continue to compete successfully. So far as shorter hours or higher pay are really used to make the artisan a better man, there is little fear but that they will also make him a better worker, and that the resources of this country will be increased rather than diminished by the change. There is, indeed, no royal road for attaining a better standard of comfort among the labourers; legislation can often prevent them from being ground down, and can perhaps insist on their having opportunities for rising; but it is only as they are inspired with better ideals, and with strength of purpose to realise them, that these opportunities will be turned to good account, and that the increasing wealth of the country will tell very decidedly on the condition not only of those who succeed in saving capital and rising in the world, but on those who continue to live by wages as well.

III. Public Debts and Danger of Accidental Extortion.

1. There are two points which may be taken into account before this long discussion is summed up. It has been pointed out above that in countries where there is much capital the owners are forced to be content with a low rate of necessary remuneration; and that the indication of this is found in their willingness to have recourse to worse soils and to increase the extent or the intensity of their cultivation, despite the fact that they are likely to get a return at a diminished rate. When there is an increase of population and more food is needed, an increase of capital and more means available for producing it—in fact, when there is material progress as it is understood in modern times—there is likely to be a diminished rate of necessary remuneration to the capitalist.

2. In some of the countries of the world material progress of this modern type has been going on for centuries; in some it is a thing of decades; in others the history can only be counted in years, and as a consequence the necessary remuneration for capital in one country, say in New Zealand, differs very much from the necessary remuneration in another, say Holland or England; and this difference has some very important consequences when we consider its influence on the distribution of capital throughout the world. Hitherto we have only had to consider the necessary remuneration and exceptional profit in one particular place; but it remains to consider what influence is exerted by varieties of necessary remuneration in different places. The necessary remuneration in New Zealand is probably nearly double what it is here; and it appears almost as easy to get 5 or 6 per cent. there as to get 3 per cent. here. The consequence is that there has been a steady drain of capital from the old countries to the new; and that men prefer to live on the proceeds of capital lent to the New Zealand Government or municipalities rather than to engage in business enterprise in this country. There is danger of capital going abroad, not because it is driven out by any occurrences here, but because it is drawn out by the large return which is offered elsewhere. This cannot be corrected by cutting down the outlay in business, but it will correct itself gradually as capital is formed in the new lands and the owners are forced to be content with a lower necessary remuneration.

3. The subject has now been dealt with in such a way that we can return to consider the danger of extortion. For purposes of illustration let us suppose that the necessary rate of remuneration in this country, in most kinds of trade, is 3 per cent. and that in New Zealand it is 5 per cent. We may then say that the man who lends money at 3 per cent. in this country or at 5 per cent. in New Zealand is only taking what he could have obtained by enterprise in either land, and that he is fully justified in asking for such a rate of return. But even so he is liable at any time to drift

into the position of an extortioner and draw a gain at the expense of others. He may have lent on mortgage in England, and owing to the agricultural depression and the fall of rents the interest on his mortgage may absorb the entire return from the estate and more. In such a case, if he is paid, he must be paid at the expense of the landlord; the money may have been sunk in making real improvements in the estate, but if there is a great fall in rent nothing may be forthcoming in consequence of the improvement; the entire loss has fallen on the owner of the estate, and the mortgagee has a legal right to exact his annual interest if he can get it anyhow. Even though the interest is so low it may accidentally become extortionate, because the lender is completely secured, and draws a moderate gain without taking any share in the risks of bad times.

In the same sort of way there may be accidental extortion in the case of loans to a foreign government. It is often the case that State-trading is expensive and badly managed, and the schemes for laying down railways and developing harbours may cost vast sums and fail to secure the direct or indirect remuneration that was hoped for. In such a case the man who has lent money at 5 per cent. has not asked an excessive rate; but if 5 per cent. is not earned, directly or indirectly, he can only obtain his interest at the expense of the colonists and out of taxes they pay. The whole burden of failure falls on them, and the lender continues to draw his interest at their expense, and by means of an increase of taxation.

4. This danger is not an imaginary one; for as capital becomes more abundant in any new country the rate of necessary remuneration is likely to decline, and there will be greater and greater difficulty in paying the interest at which capital was originally borrowed. Even if statesmen were perfectly wise, and if all public borrowing were for the sake of making remunerative works, there would be danger that the burden of the original interest would be increasingly felt, unless it could be readjusted by some financial operation like Mr. Goschen's. But statesmen are not all perfectly

wise, and the public debts of the world are not all incurred for remunerative purposes; there is a constantly increasing burden of interest which has to be defrayed by taxation, and which must have most serious results on the industry and commerce of the world. Of the total annual produce of the world, in 1882, something like £200,000,000 was not divided between the labourer who works and the capitalist who conducts the enterprise, but went as a fixed charge to those who had lent capital in times gone by; while much of the principal has been wasted or extravagantly used, the burden of interest has still to be defrayed.

5. The exhaustion of the provinces under the Roman Republic is so far analogous to the pressure which is exerted by foreign bondholders in the present day, that it is at least incumbent on us to look carefully at the state of the case, and see if it is practicable to check the evils which sapped the strength of the greatest power of ancient times. It is at all events possible for the scrupulous man to avoid having any personal part in this matter by abstaining from this mode of employing capital altogether; or, if that seems impracticable, the risk of accidental extortion will be reduced to the lowest possible point, if he only lends to very wealthy countries and for a low rate of return.

The pressure of extortion, whether through demands for interest out of taxation, or through saving outlay by grinding down the labourer, will show itself in injury to national resources. It may be the exhaustion of the soil or the mines, as under the Roman rule; it may be in the degradation and weakening of the population. It is a real danger which only ceases to be serious when it is faced and kept in view. There may be legislative interference to check the grinding down of the labouring population, and there has been; but it may be doubted if legislation can check the evil which may occur through reckless borrowing by a Government and subsequent exhaustion to meet the demands for interest. A bargain is a bargain, and no man and no Government is justified in repudiating an agreement because the bargain has turned out badly, especially if the mischief has lain in their own folly. But the man of probity and good sense may well scruple to lend his capital to a Government in terms which may lead to his drawing interest in a fashion which exhausts and impoverishes the country where his money is placed.

CHAPTER XIV.

THE ENJOYMENT OF WEALTH.

I. Right and Wrong in Enjoyment.

HERE it seems that the task we had set ourselves might be brought to a close. We have examined the part which capital plays in modern society, the dangers which arise in connexion with it, and the manner in which it is being administered, and is likely to be, so far as we can look forward. We have tried to look at capital in itself, to see how it is formed, and how replaced, to note the nature of the service it renders to the public, and the character of its relation with the labourer. We have touched, too, on the considerations which should guide a man as to the direction in which he uses his capital, and the manner in which he bargains for a return ; and thus have examined personal duty in regard to social life. It is by the manner he uses his wealth, and the manner he gets his income, that the capitalist is brought into contact and exercises a direct influence on society at large; but it is not unnecessary to add a few remarks on the duties of private life as well—on the manner in which a man enjoys his wealth. For no man lives to himself alone, and there is a very real, if not very easily measurable, influence which the personal and private life of each exercises on the well-being of others.

1. After all, the prospective enjoyment of wealth is never left out of sight altogether; even the miser looks forward to a continued enjoyment of the sight of his accumulations. It is for the sake of enjoying freedom from anxiety that some

men form a hoard and save capital; it is for the sake of enjoying wealth that others enter into business and try to increase their income. The special ideas of enjoyment which any man cherishes, and for which he provides, are constantly before him; the aims he has in view may affect his conduct in regard to the means he uses for attaining them, and they will at any rate affect the feelings with which other people regard his success. If he is merely vicious in his ideas of enjoyment they will grudge him his gain, while the man who has been generous and wise in the use of his wealth will find ready and hearty sympathy on all sides if he loses it. When we look at the character of personal life, and the manner of enjoying wealth, we may see that they are not merely matters of private duty, but that they have a real bearing on the condition of society at large.

2. Stress has been laid above on the importance of work; and it has been asserted that according to Christian conceptions of duty the ideal for man is not a life of idleness but a life of work. It is this that will call forth the best of his powers, and that will enable him to benefit his fellowmen; and it is when we keep this conception of life clearly before us that we advance one step towards discriminating in regard to what is right and wrong in the enjoyment of wealth. If man is primarily a worker, he is the better of all such enjoyment as keeps him up to his best as a worker; he is the better for such rest as recuperates him after work, and for such recreation as refreshes him and fits him for doing his work better. These are elements both of rest and recreation which it is positively right for him to enjoy; such rest and such recreation, according to his powers and temperament, as keep him at his best, and enable him over a period of years to do the most he is capable of, are times of idleness and amusement which no one need grudge him.

3. On the other hand, there can be no doubt that any enjoyment of wealth which unfits a man for work is wrong. If he takes a long holiday and gets into easy-going and irregular habits, so as to be unable to settle down again to the routine of ordinary duty and the monotonous round of

daily tasks, his idleness has been wrong. If his recreation takes the form of a 'wet night,' so that he finds himself a 'bit chippy' in the morning and unfit for work, his recreation has been wrong. Any form of enjoyment which fits a man for his work is right, and any form of enjoyment which unfits a man for his work is wrong. The one is recreation since it recreates his energies, the other is dissipation since it dissipates them.

These distinctions may be found to include a larger number of cases than might at first sight appear, but they can of course only be applied personally. What is necessary rest for one would be gross idleness for another; what would amuse one and prove suitable recreation would bore another man to death. Still, the man of forty, who is not a fool, will have a very good idea as to what is rest and recreation for him, and what is idleness and dissipation; he will be able to judge how things affect his powers of working. There may be a large number of enjoyments, however, to which it is difficult to apply this test; they seem to be things indifferent, as we cannot see that they have much bearing one way or another on powers of work. But after all, the duty of work is only one side of human life, and diligence only one part of human duty, and we may be able to test other enjoyments by their bearing upon other sides of human character.

4. Any use of wealth that facilitates the development of any kind of skill or the refinement of taste has much to be said for it; at all events wealth is not wasted if it promotes the cultivation of human faculties, intellectual or artistic. Enjoyment in connexion with the pursuit of knowledge or the practice of any branch of art is in itself wholesome and good; and this is true of athletic games which improve the human body, as well as of any intellectual exercise which disciplines and improves the mind. On the other hand, there may be over-indulgence which mars rather than develops the mental and bodily powers,—a strain which exhausts the physique and plants the seeds of disease; and while enjoyments which develop faculty and power are good

so far as they go, enjoyments which exhaust the body or deteriorate the mind are obviously wrong.

5. Man, however, is a social being, and it is a poor thing for him to aim only at his personal self-development; he may indeed have his reward and become the complete prig. It is far better if he can aim at mixing happily with other men, can learn to appreciate their excellence, to sympathise with their interests, and to make allowance for their faults; because as part of a social circle his life is more complete than when he has no thought for anything but himself, and neglects all opportunity of correcting his one-sidedness, and of learning from the experience of others. And thus to mix and learn from others involves the expenditure of time and money in social enjoyments; in fact, it is in connexion with entertainment that there is the most frequent temptation to extravagance. It might at least be kept within bounds if the host would always recollect that anything that is bad for him is probably bad for his guests, and that mere display for the sake of showing off is at best a vulgar pleasure. To cut down eating and drinking to the limits required by moderation, and which really conduce to pleasant social intercourse, would be no small gain, and would mean a considerable retrenchment of wasteful and injurious enjoyment of wealth.

II. The Neglect of Opportunities and Waste of Wealth.

1. In thus trying to mark out the modes of enjoyment which are wrong from those that are not, one may add that in so far as the owners use wealth so as to injure themselves and others in person and character, or so as merely to gratify a petty vanity by idly displaying it, there is ample reason for the indignation which is felt in regard to the luxurious expenditure of the rich. When ball decorations involve an expenditure of £1000 on flowers there is an outlay which is wrong; not because it is unproductive consumption, but because it is a wrong kind of unproductive consumption, and is an idle display. It is extravagance like this that is to blame for setting class against class; jealousy itself finds

little to fasten on in the case of a wealthy man who uses his wealth wisely and well, but it is aroused by evidences of extravagance and dissipation; and when aroused it is ready to condemn everything that it cannot appreciate.

2. There are some in the present day whose sense of justice is violated by the inequalities of life, and who cannot reconcile themselves to that state of affairs where some enjoy so very much and others have so very little. But those who feel that communism is impracticable, and who, while they welcome every sort of effort at levelling up, fear that any attempt at levelling down would be a hindrance to future progress, must force themselves to accept inequalities in human life, as there are inequalities in other spheres. Those who take this standpoint will not be unduly severe in their criticisms of any man's expenditure so long as it is clear that he is not injuring himself and his property, and is getting his money's worth in something that is relatively permanent. If he is not unfitting himself for the duties of life, if he is cultivating his bodily and mental powers, if he is enjoying genial intercourse with men of kindred tastes and forming ties of friendship with his neighbours, there will be but few to grudge him his wealth. It is the man who might have done all these things and does none of them, who has all the opportunities which wealth affords and throws them away, who is a mere idler, careless of anything but his own pleasure, and whose pleasures render him feebler in body and emptier in mind, it is such misuse of wealth that rightly rouses scorn and indignation. For all misuse of opportunities is bad, and the greater the opportunities are, the more shameful is the conduct of those who waste them.

III. **The Sacrifice of Enjoyment in its bearing on Material Progress.**

But even those who have not misused their wealth at all, who have had their money's worth in the best that a high civilisation can afford, who have been diligent in the duties that came to hand, and have made the most of every opportunity by developing their own powers and tastes and cultivating the friendship of others, have not attained to the best standard in the use of wealth. There is higher virtue, a virtue that is found not in enjoyment but in sacrifice.

1. There is the sacrifice that is involved in using wealth for others, that is the outward embodiment of care and consideration for the failures of life. Indiscriminate charity is good so far as it goes; it shows a real if a somewhat spasmodic sympathy with suffering. Discriminating relief is better still, for it shows a more thoughtful care for the needs of others, and marks the man who is at pains that his help shall be given where it helps most. Preventive charity is best of all since it sets itself to diagnose the conditions which lead to poverty and attacks them in their beginning; it shows the greatest readiness to give time and thought to the sufferings of others. But in whatever way there is an effort to reduce the inequalities and mitigate the sufferings of human life, there is an effort which may be welcomed even if it be misdirected. Misdirected charity may do harm; it may encourage dishonesty and hypocrisy and idleness, and all sorts of evils. But the man who stays his hand until he is absolutely certain his charity is well directed and cannot do any possible harm, will not find that he responds to many calls. Charity hopeth all things, and there are many cases when the sufferer may well have the benefit of the doubt. The poor are improvident and drink; the rich indulge their vanity by silly ostentation. So long as so much money is wasted, and wasted in so many ways, why should the petty extravagances of the poor be so loudly blamed? To put it on the lowest grounds, if somebody is going to make ducks and drakes of the money, why should the poor never have the fun of trying their hand at the game? For after all, no human being can do much more for another than to give him opportunities; no human being can compel another to use them aright. And those who have, may well sacrifice a portion of their possessions by using it, not for enjoyment of any kind, but to give better opportunities of education and work and comfort to others.

In the progress of society there are many who are left behind in the race through no fault of their own, whose power of work is superseded by machinery, or whose health breaks down under the strain of the struggle. And while we cannot wish to raise artificial barriers or stay the pace at which material progress advances, we ought to feel that it is incumbent on those who are succeeding, or have succeeded, to be mindful of others who have been less fortunate. To be mindful, too, of those who are starting in the race of life, and to see that they are as well equipped as may be for the course they have to run. To insist on equal opportunities for all to start alike seems vain, and to attempt to carry this out compulsorily would be disastrous. But to reduce the existing inequalities and to afford improved opportunities to all is worth aiming at, and this can be accomplished by the sacrifice of enjoyment and the generous use of wealth.

2. Such sacrifice may tend to remove the inequalities of society, but it will not tend to raise society itself. For that we must have an aim which rises above the present possibilities of enjoyment altogether; we must cherish a better ideal than they can afford. There is an absolute limit to the increase and enrichment of man upon the globe, but there are definite possibilities of advance in capacity and self-command and all that makes man noble. And those who cherish an ideal for themselves and for the race (formed in terms not of what man has but of what he may himself be), and who are trying to realise it in their own persons, are giving the best guidance to their generation for possible steps in progress. They are setting before us, not the means by which material wealth may be increased, but a clearer view of the objects for which it may be most worthily used, because a better view of what man himself may be. As the heroes of every cause are ready to sacrifice life for the aim they set before them, so have they shown themselves ready to sacrifice every present enjoyment and to keep themselves free from every material interest in order to maintain their ideal of a better, less selfish, and purer human life. They have cultivated their powers, not by enjoying all the opportunities that came to hand, but by trying to live without such

things and learning to live above them. And they have not lived in vain; the world owes much to the inventors and discoverers, it owes more to ascetics and saints. There have been men in all ages who have taught their fellow-men how to overcome nature and to acquire wealth; there have been others who have showed them how to overcome themselves, to rise to a better conception of man's life, and thus to use their wealth so that it might tend to human welfare.

Typography by J. S. Cushing & Co., Boston.

Presswork by Berwick & Smith, Boston.

UNIVERSITY EXTENSION MANUALS

A NEW SERIES OF
USEFUL AND IMPORTANT BOOKS

EDITED BY PROFESSOR WM. KNIGHT

Each, 12mo, $1.00, Net

CHARLES SCRIBNER'S SONS, Publishers

THIS Series, to be published by John Murray in England and Charles Scribner's Sons in America, is the outgrowth of the University Extension movement, and is designed to supply the need so widely felt of authorized books for study and reference both by students and by the general public.

The aim of these Manuals is to educate rather than to inform. In their preparation, details will be avoided except when they illustrate the working of general laws and the development of principles ; while the historical evolution of both the literary and scientific subjects, as well as their philosophical significance, will be kept in view.

The remarkable success which has attended University Extension in England has been largely due to the union of scientific with popular treatment, and of simplicity with thoroughness.

This movement, however, can only reach those resident in the larger centres of population, while all over the country there are thoughtful persons who desire the same kind of teaching. It is for them also that this Series is designed. Its aim is to supply the general reader with the same kind of teaching as is given in lectures, and to reflect the spirit which has characterized the movement, viz., the combination of principles with facts and of methods with results.

The Manuals are also intended to be contributions to the literature of the subjects with which they respectively deal quite apart from University Extension; and some of them will be found to meet a general rather than a special want.

They will be issued simultaneously in England and America. Volumes dealing with separate sections of Literature, Science, Philosophy, History, and Art, have been assigned to representative literary men, to University Professors, or to Extension Lecturers connected with Oxford, Cambridge, London, and the Universities of Scotland and Ireland.

NOW READY

THE USE AND ABUSE OF MONEY

By Dr. W. Cunningham, Trinity College, Cambridge. 12mo, $1.00, *net.*

CONTENTS—POLITICAL ECONOMY WITH ASSUMPTIONS AND WITHOUT — INDUSTRY WITHOUT CAPITAL — CAPITALIST ERA — MATERIAL PROGRESS AND MORAL INDIFFERENCE—THE CONTROL OF CAPITAL—THE FORMATION OF CAPITAL—THE INVESTMENT OF CAPITAL — CAPITAL IN ACTION — THE REPLACEMENT OF CAPITAL—THE DIRECTION OF CAPITAL—PERSONAL RESPONSIBILITY—DUTY IN REGARD TO EMPLOYING CAPITAL—DUTY IN REGARD TO THE RETURNS ON CAPITAL—THE ENJOYMENT OF WEALTH.

Dr. Cunningham's book is intended for those who are already familiar with the outlines of the subject, and is meant to help them to think on topics about which everybody talks. It is essentially a popular treatise, and the headings of the three parts, Social Problems, Practical Questions, and Personal Duty, give a broad view of the large scope of the book. The subject is Capital in its relation to Social Progress, and the title emphasizes the element of personal responsibility that enters into the questions raised. The discussion is as thorough as it is practical, the author's main purpose being to enlighten the lay reader. The novelty of his point of view and the clearness of his style unite to make the book both interesting and valuable. The volume contains a syllabus of subjects and a list of books for reference for the use of those who may wish to pursue the study further.

THE FINE ARTS

By G. BALDWIN BROWN, Professor of Fine Arts in the University of Edinburgh. 12mo, with Illustrations, $1.00, *net.*

CONTENTS—Part I.—ART AS THE EXPRESSION OF POPULAR FEELINGS AND IDEALS:—THE BEGINNINGS OF ART—THE FESTIVAL IN ITS RELATION TO THE FORM AND SPIRIT OF CLASSICAL ART—MEDIÆVAL FLORENCE AND HER PAINTERS. Part II.—THE FORMAL CONDITIONS OF ARTISTIC EXPRESSION : — SOME ELEMENTS OF EFFECT IN THE ARTS OF FORM—THE WORK OF ART AS SIGNIFICANT — THE WORK OF ART AS BEAUTIFUL. Part III.—THE ARTS OF FORM :—ARCHITECTURAL BEAUTY IN RELATION TO CONSTRUCTION—THE CONVENTIONS OF SCULPTURE —PAINTING OLD AND NEW.

The whole field of the fine-arts of painting, sculpture and architecture, their philosophy, function and historic accomplishment, is covered in Professor Baldwin Brown's compact but exhaustive manual. The work is divided into three parts, the first considering art as the expression of popular feelings and ideas— a most original investigation of the origin and development of the aesthetic impulse ; the second discussing the formal conditions of artistic expression ; and the third treating the "arts of form" in their theory and practice and giving a luminous exposition of the significance of the great historic movements in architecture, sculpture and painting from the earliest times to the present.

THE PHILOSOPHY OF THE BEAUTIFUL

Being the Outlines of the History of Aesthetics. By WILLIAM KNIGHT, Professor of Philosophy in the University of St. Andrews. 12mo, $1.00, *net.*

CONTENTS — INTRODUCTORY — PREHISTORIC ORIGINS — ORIENTAL ART AND SPECULATION—THE PHILOSOPHY OF GREECE

—THE NEOPLATONISTS—THE GRAECO-ROMAN PERIOD—MEDIAE-
VALISM — THE PHILOSOPHY OF GERMANY — OF FRANCE — OF
ITALY—OF HOLLAND—OF BRITAIN—OF AMERICA.

Not content with presenting an historical sketch of past opinion and tendency on the subject of the Beautiful, Prof. Knight
shows how these philosophical theories have been evolved, how
they have been the outcome of social as well as of intellectual
causes, and have often been the product of obscure phenomena
in the life of a nation. Thus a deep human interest is given to
his synopsis of speculative thought on the subject of Beauty and
to his analysis of the art school corresponding to each period
from the time of the Egyptians down to the present day. He
traces the sequence of opinion in each country as expressed in its
literature and its art works, and shows how doctrines of art are
based upon theories of Beauty,' and how these theories often have
their roots in the customs of society itself.

ENGLISH COLONIZATION AND EMPIRE

By ALFRED CALDECOTT, St. John's College, Cambridge. 12mo, with Maps and Diagrams, $1.00,
net.

CONTENTS—PIONEER PERIOD—INTERNATIONAL STRUGGLE
—DEVELOPMENT AND SEPARATION OF AMERICA—THE ENGLISH
IN INDIA—RECONSTRUCTION AND FRESH DEVELOPMENT—GOV-
ERNMENT OF THE EMPIRE—TRADE AND TRADE POLICY—SUPPLY
OF LABOR—NATIVE RACES—EDUCATION AND RELIGION—GEN-
ERAL REFLECTIONS—BOOKS OF REFERENCE.

The diffusion of European, and, more particularly, of English,
civilization over the face of the inhabited and habitable world is
the subject of this book. The treatment of this great theme covers
the origin and the historical, political, economical and ethnological
development of the English colonies, the moral, intellectual, industrial and social aspects of the question being also considered.
There is thus spread before the reader a bird's-eye view of the
British colonies, great and small, from their origin until the present
time, with a summary of the wars and other great events which
have occurred in the progress of this colonizing work, and with
a careful examination of some of the most important questions,
economical, commercial and political, which now affect the relation of the colonies and the parent nation. The maps and diagrams are an instructive and valuable addition to the book.

IN PREPARATION

FRENCH LITERATURE. By H. G. KEENE.

THE REALM OF NATURE. With Maps and Illustrations. By HUGH R. MILL, University of Edinburgh.

THE STUDY OF ANIMAL LIFE. By T. ARTHUR THOMSON, University of Edinburgh.

THE DAILY LIFE OF THE GREEKS AND THE ROMANS. By W. ANDERSON, Oriel College, Oxford.

THE ELEMENTS OF ETHICS. By JOHN H. MUIRHEAD, Balliol College, Oxford.

OUTLINES OF ENGLISH LITERATURE. By WILLIAM RENTON, University of St. Andrews.

SHAKESPEARE AND HIS PREDECESSORS IN THE ENGLISH DRAMA. By F. S. BOAS, Balliol College, Oxford.

THE FRENCH REVOLUTION. By C. E. MALLEY, Balliol College, Oxford.

LOGIC, INDUCTIVE AND DEDUCTIVE. By WILLIAM MINTO, University of Aberdeen.

THE HISTORY OF ASTRONOMY. By ARTHUR BERRY, King's College, Cambridge.

THE ENGLISH POETS, FROM BLAKE TO TENNYSON. By the Rev. STOPFORD A. BROOKE, Trinity College, Dublin.

ENERGY IN NATURE. An Introduction to Physical Science. By JOHN COX, Trinity College, Cambridge.

OUTLINES OF MODERN BOTANY. By Prof. PATRICK GEDDES, University College, Dundee.

THE JACOBEAN POETS. By EDMUND GOSSE, Trinity College, Cambridge.

TEXT BOOK OF THE HISTORY OF EDUCATION. By Prof. SIMON S. LAURIE, University of Edinburgh.

BRITISH DOMINION IN INDIA. By Sir ALFRED LYALL, K. C. B., K. C. S. I.

THE PHYSIOLOGY OF THE SENSES. By Prof. McKENDRICK, University of Glasgow, and Dr. SNODGRASS, Physiological Laboratory, Glasgow.

COMPARATIVE RELIGION. By Prof. MENZIES, University of St. Andrews.

THE ENGLISH NOVEL FROM ITS ORIGIN TO SIR WALTER SCOTT. By Prof. RALEIGH, University College, Liverpool.

STUDIES IN MODERN GEOLOGY. By Dr. R. D. ROBERTS, Clare College, Cambridge.

PROBLEMS OF POLITICAL ECONOMY. By M. E. SADLER, Senior Student of Christ Church, Oxford.

PSYCHOLOGY: A HISTORICAL SKETCH. By Prof. SETH, University of St. Andrews.

MECHANICS. By Prof. JAMES STUART, M. P., Trinity College, Cambridge.

THE GREAT EDUCATORS.

Edited by Nicholas Murray Butler, Ph.D. Sold separately. Each vol., 12mo, net, $1.00.

A series of volumes giving concise, comprehensive accounts of the leading movements in educational thought, grouped about the personalities that have influenced them. The treatment of each theme is to be individual and biographic as well as institutional. The writers are well-known students of education, and it is expected that the series, when completed, will furnish a genetic account of ancient education, the rise of the Christian schools, the foundation and growth of universities, and that the great modern movements suggested by the names of the Jesuit Order, Rousseau, Pestalozzi, Froebel, Herbart, Dr. Arnold and Horace Mann, will be adequately described and criticised.

ARISTOTLE, and the Ancient Educational Ideals. By Thomas Davidson, M.A., LL.D. *Nearly Ready.*

ALCUIN, and the Rise of the Christian Schools. By Andrew F. West, Ph.D., Professor of Latin and Pedagogics in Princeton University. *Nearly Ready.*

ABELARD, and the Origin and Early History of Universities. By Jules Gabriel Compayré, Rector of the Academy of Poitiers, France. *Nearly Ready.*

LOYOLA, and the Educational System of the Jesuits. By Rev. Thomas Hughes, S. J., of Detroit College. *Ready.*

PESTALOZZI; or, the Friend and Student of Children. By J. G. Fitch, LL.D., Her Majesty's Inspector of Schools. *In Preparation.*

FROEBEL. By H. Courthope Bowen, M.A., Lecturer on Education in the University of Cambridge. *In Preparation.*

HORACE MANN; or, Public Education in the United States. By the Editor. *In Preparation.*

Other volumes on "Rousseau; or, Education According to Nature," "Herbart; or, Modern German Education," and on "Thomas Arnold; or, the English Education of To-day," are in preparation.

CHARLES SCRIBNER'S SONS, Publishers,
743 & 745 Broadway, New York.

www.ingramcontent.com/pod-product-compliance
Lightning Source LLC
Chambersburg PA
CBHW020055030726
47498CB00006B/1805